The Children of Skylark Ward

For Helen and Michael

The Children of Skylark Ward

Teaching severely handicapped children

ANN HALES

CAMBRIDGE UNIVERSITY PRESS

Cambridge
London   New York   Melbourne

582240

Published by the Syndics of the Cambridge University Press
The Pitt Building, Trumpington Street, Cambridge CB2 IRP
Bentley House, 200 Euston Road, London NW1 2DB
32 East 57th Street, New York, NY 10022, USA
296 Beaconsfield Parade, Middle Park, Melbourne 3206, Australia

© Cambridge University Press 1978

First published 1978

Printed in Great Britain by
Cox & Wyman Ltd
London, Fakenham and Reading

Library of Congress Cataloguing in Publication Data
Hales, Ann, 1926–
The children of skylark ward.
Bibliography: p.
Includes index.
1. Handicapped children – Education. I. Title.
L'C4015.H27   371.9   77–80836
ISBN 0 521 21752 0

CONTENTS

ACKNOWLEDGEMENTS

The poem 'The caged skylark' is from the fourth edition (1967) of *The poems of Gerard Manley Hopkins*, edited by W. H. Gardner and N. H. Mackenzie, published by Oxford University Press, by arrangement with the Society of Jesus. It is reproduced by kind permission of Oxford University Press.

The photograph on page 50 was taken by Freddie Collins and is reproduced with his permission.

PREFACE

This is the story of the three years I spent teaching a group of severely physically and mentally handicapped children, in a classroom of a hospital ward.

It is a highly personalised account of this experience. In order to preserve the children's privacy and anonymity, and to avoid causing any unwitting hurt to their parents, or to anyone else concerned with them, I have altered names, ages, sexes and some of the characteristics of the children and of the adults involved, so that the resulting profiles are not of any particular existing person. I have tried to do this in ways which will not invalidate the book as an account of life with a group of multiply handicapped children.

The description of the ways in which we tried to teach the children to develop, and to learn through play, is, I hope, an accurate one. The book has been written in the hope that some of the ideas will be useful to others who are caring for similar children – as parents, as nurses and as teachers. I hope it is a positive book, but one that does not underestimate the exacting nature of the work, or of the burdens that the children, and those who love them, must carry.

What we did with the children was a team effort. As the teacher I was responsible for the classroom teaching – the mistakes and omissions were mine. The credit for any success we had must be shared among many people, especially the young teacher of the group under whom I worked as a voluntary helper, before taking over the group. I could never have started, or carried on the job, without the experience and unfailing encouragement of my head teacher who is a continual source of strength and inspiration to all who work in that hospital school. During my second year with the class I was joined by a classroom assistant. From then on we worked as a partnership, and it was Elizabeth who thought up many of the new ways in which we worked with the children, especially in the group activities.

During my time in the classroom the ward was looked after by three successive charge nurses. Their devotion to the children, in working conditions far harder than mine, and their unfailing co-operation and friendship, made my role a very happy and satisfying one. So much of what I learnt about the children came directly from our team of hospital physiotherapists. Because a teacher and a physiotherapist must have similar goals for this kind of child, I explore our relationship in more depth in a later chapter (see page 48).

In the book I single out various members of ward staff who made a particular contribution in the classroom; there were many others including ward domestics, junior aids, nursing auxiliaries, nurses, students and volunteers, who by relating to individual children in their own different ways taught everyone else something new about the children.

I have called the ward 'Skylark' for many reasons. The hospital was in the country. In the spring and summer, skylarks soared up from the fields beside the ward. We encouraged the children to watch the upward flight of these insignificant brown birds, and to listen to their singing. Unconsciously I found myself saying lines from Shelley's 'To a Skylark'. The more I thought about this poem, the more I found ideas that expressed, most perfectly, what I felt about the children and their relationships to us.

The hospital was set in a dip among gently rolling fields which grew corn and bright yellow mustard crops. I drove out there in the morning straight towards the rising sun. Often as I went home westwards in the evening, totally exhausted, there would be a marvellous sunset, and thinking of the children I had left behind, I would find myself saying:

> In the golden lightning
> Of the sunken sun,
> O'er which the clouds are bright'ning,
> Thou dost float and run;
> Like an unbodied joy whose race is just begun.

The more I grew to know and love the children, the more they seemed to be people with spirits like yours and mine, but fettered by an accident of nature in bodies and minds unlike yours and mine. As human beings there was so much more that united than divided us. I look forward to the time when they will be released from their fetters. What is really important for us as unfettered people comes in the final line of the poem: 'The world should listen then – as I am listening now.'

Chapter 1

SETTING THE SCENE

To set the scene for Skylark Ward, I will describe, briefly, the structure of the hospital and the school within it.

The hospital was opened ten years ago and houses about 300 severely mentally handicapped people. There are a few old people, but basically the hospital takes in children and adults up to about fifty years of age, with IQs in the 0–50 range. Some of the patients have severe behavioural disorders in addition to severe subnormality.

Some are semi-ambulant and need wheelchairs to get about the hospital and its grounds. Most patients in the hospital go each day to an occupational therapy department, a special training unit or to the school.

At the time of writing, two of the thirty-bed wards look after sixty children and young adults who suffer severe physical as well as mental handicap – Skylark was one of these wards, the other was Kestrel.

Most of the children under the age of eighteen went to school, and a few came as day pupils from the community. The school took about 120 children, but the number was never constant as a child coming in for short-term care (STC) or special assessment, even babies of two months, would usually come into the care of a teacher during some, or for all, of the regular school hours.

The school for most of the children was in a separate building, but not for those from Skylark. Because of the distance involved they were too handicapped for it to be practicable to transport them there. There was also another small, special assessment unit which, like Skylark Ward, had its own full-time teacher, classroom assistant and junior aid (a seventeen- to eighteen-year-old girl, employed by the hospital and often filling in a year or so before becoming a nursing auxiliary or starting formal training as a nurse).

The children on Kestrel Ward were able to be wheeled or carried into the school as their ward was just beside the school building. This meant there were, in effect, two special care units – one for the Kestrel children situated in a large school classroom, the other at the opposite end of the spacious hospital grounds, on Skylark Ward. The school staff running the two units had similar problems to face in teaching their kind of pupil and often discussed these together. Each special care unit had its own advantages and disadvantages. The Kestrel children going from their ward into the school had the stimulation of a twice-daily change of environment – they went back to the ward for lunch and were able to share the general atmosphere of going to school with other, less-handicapped children. As their classroom was a permanent one, the maximum amount of stimulating equipment, visual aids, etc. could be kept, and the children were already on the spot for any activity that involved the whole school.

School for children on Skylark only meant going at regular times from Monday to Friday into an ordinary ward dayroom which had been especially prepared for them, for those hours only, with suitable school equipment and an abundance of toys and play materials. School-time for them was heralded by the arrival and departure of their teacher and her assistant, and was focused much more on special people and very much less on *physical surroundings* than it was for the Kestrel children.

I felt the Skylark children missed out on the change of surroundings and, as school staff, we had to make strenuous efforts to make up for this by taking them out of doors, or to school functions whenever the weather, available help and circumstances allowed this. Being taught on the ward may have benefited them in that all the people caring for them, both in and out of school hours, formed an integrated

2

network. Ward staff, including domestics, came into the classroom for brief periods and helped, or played with the children – particularly twice a day when the children had their mid-morning and mid-afternoon drinks. Parents, relations and friends who happened to visit during school hours always came into the classroom, probably more often than did the Kestrel parents. As the teacher on the ward, I had opportunities for very close liaison with the charge nurse and all other staff, which certainly made the roles of myself and my assistant different from that of our colleagues in the school special care unit. Kestrel school staff had very good relationships with the Kestrel nursing staff and went in and out of that ward at least four times each school day to fetch and carry, but their degree of integration on the ward could not be exactly as ours was on Skylark.

One of the extra burdens of the Skylark classroom arrangement was the business of having to set out and put away the school equipment daily. An advantage of this was the opportunity to think out fresh patterns of room arrangement. A drawback was the knowledge that anything, including paintings on the walls, left around out of school hours might disappear, or get damaged by some boisterous semi-mobile patient over the weekend.

However, we *were* lucky, in that our very large L-shaped room faced south and west, had enormous windows and a high ceiling, so that it felt spacious and caught every scrap of daylight and sunlight that was available. Two large wall areas were covered in softboard so that we could mount paintings and other visual material. Double doors opened out on to a roofed terrace and we had easy access to a garden.

I and my assistant, Elizabeth, were employed by the local education authority. Our day always began in the school building. Here we had staff meetings before school began at 9 a.m.; we collected the class register and supplies of paint, paper or other special equipment; we heard who might be visiting us that day, learnt if we had a student nurse placement with us, and whether there were any special activities

3

going on in school to which we could send a few of our more able children. We returned to school at lunchtime and again at 4 p.m. at the end of the school day, for a cup of tea with the rest of the school staff. During school hours we were visited daily by the head, or her deputy, and several times a week by one of the two music teachers, and the physiotherapists who were based in the school building.

Despite all this contact with school, teaching on Skylark gave one a feeling of being in a remote outpost. It was very difficult, at times, to get across to ward staff that I and my assistant were on the ward to *educate* the children, and not just to organise a well-stocked playroom with recreational activities which they could all, to some extent, enjoy! Some members of the ward staff found the concept of *education*, training and learning through play, very hard to grasp. In a sense the more my assistant and I identified with the nursing staff, doing things above our normal teaching duties, like changing children when the ward was short-staffed, helping out voluntarily at the odd lunchtime, the harder it was for them to see us as 'school', and the more they saw us as part of the Skylark caring team.

When Elizabeth and I arrived on Skylark in the morning we often found the children still having breakfast. Having greeted the children and talked briefly to whoever was in charge and discovered whether any child was too ill to come into school that day, we hurried through into our room. Our first task was to arrange it while the children were being washed and changed by the ward staff. On our way down to Skylark from the school we would have discussed our plans for the day and would immediately set out the room according to our programme.

We covered the large plastic central mattress (roughly twelve feet square) with clean sheets. In the centre we arranged rubber car tyres and a stack of Cell Barnes foam rubber shapes in which the children might sit, crawl and roll. For a group activity we set out at one end of the room four small tables and chairs with sag bags for the more physically

4

disabled children. We would get out the sand or water trough and put chairs round this. We covered two smaller mattresses with sheets – one near a long mirror, one perhaps inside a tent. We set up a seesaw, and if we had any active short-term care children we might put out a swing, a slide and a rocking boat. We hung fresh toys from the net over the mattress and set out toys all over the floor and table surfaces.

All this preparation, which we had to do at top speed, before the children arrived, was directed towards making the room into something different for them. A place to which they could come with a feeling of excited anticipation; a place in which they knew they would be welcomed individually and find new things to do, and people ready to give them personal attention in individual activities or as part of a group achieving a clear-cut goal.

As each child arrived we aimed to talk individually to him or her for several minutes and then take him to a pre-arranged activity so that he had something to do, or to play with, until the whole group had assembled. This business of welcoming each child on arrival in the classroom, and spending a little time with him, was very important. It was a help to us that the children tended to arrive at intervals. The kind of personal attention we gave each child at this point varied. If the nursing staff were very pressed for time we might take a child straight to our long classroom mirror, get a brush and comb and spend a few moments admiring her clothes, finishing off her dressing, fetching a cardigan if we felt she was cold, doing her hair; making her aware from the start of school time that she was special and individual. This whole welcoming process might take us up to about 10 a.m., by which time every child would be using a toy, interacting with another child, or watching us getting a group activity ready for them. At this stage we might arrange a bowl of flowers or green branches, getting each child to feel, touch and smell them as we decorated the room.

Chapter 2

THE CHILDREN

The school group consisted of seventeen children, officially classed as educationally subnormal severe – ESN(S). To these were added, from time to time, short-term care children, who came in for two or more weeks' assessment on medical, psychological, social and educational grounds. Children arrived sometimes as a result of family crisis or breakdown, and we also had a number who came in regularly, especially during the summer months, to give their families holiday relief for two weeks. These were also assessed while they were with us.

The chronological ages of the children in the regular school group was two to eighteen years.[1] Among the short-term care children we sometimes had babies of under a year old. There is a section about very handicapped babies later in the book (page 88).

The group could be roughly described as consisting of severely brain-damaged children with very severe physical disabilities. One child was a mongol. One suffered from brain damage due to a rare metabolic imbalance. Three children had had meningitis or encephalitis in early infancy leading to permanent brain damage. One child was the survivor of undiagnosed twins, the other being still-born, another was a twin with a normal sibling. Most of the remainder had suffered injury during pregnancy and/or delivery: concussion because of over-precipitate delivery; oxygen starvation during prolonged, difficult labour; the umbilical cord tied tightly round the throat causing asphyxia. In some instances the causes of the subnormality had never been clearly diagnosed. Some children had had

6

difficult forceps deliveries or were born prematurely. A number of the mothers had toxaemia during pregnancy.

The pattern of these children's subsequent development was similar. Many were from birth very poor feeders, finding it difficult to suck easily. They were very slow to reach the usual 'milestones' of a normal baby's development: easy feeding, smiling, grasping and reaching out for things, sitting, crawling, standing and walking. Only one child could utter a few recognisable single words. Many could not sit unsupported; only three were semi-ambulant. Two were totally blind, three had very impaired vision, some were only partially sighted. Two were totally deaf, many had impaired hearing. Practically all the children had cerebral palsy which is the result of damage to the motor areas of the brain, occurring prior to, at, or fairly soon after birth. This affected all or parts of the children's bodies, resulting in a poor ability to execute or co-ordinate normal movements. The varying degrees of spasticity made their limbs stiff and contracted, or resulted in low muscle tone which made them very floppy.

As a further result of the brain damage, nearly all had started having convulsions at an early age; where these had continued the children became epileptics. Despite the use of controlling drugs nearly all the children had mild or severe epileptic fits. One of the side-effects of the drugs was to make them very sleepy much of the time.

In addition to this school group the ward looked after a further ten severely handicapped young adults aged between twenty and thirty years.

All the children and young adults needed full 'nursing' care. With one or two exceptions they were unable to do anything for themselves. Most were doubly incontinent.

It so happened that the Skylark school group contained more younger children than the Kestrel school group. It also seemed that the Skylark children were, with some exceptions, much more physically attractive than the Kestrel children. In the detailed profiles of eight of the Skylark children which follow, readers may ask themselves whether the

7

children were really as beautiful, as handsome or as pretty as my descriptions indicate. In fact, it so happened that they were, whereas the young adults on Skylark ward were much less physically attractive; some were ugly, if not grotesque.

Maybe research will prove, sometime, that the earlier adults start to interact actively and continuously with severely handicapped children, the more alert the children's faces will become. The more you are loved and cared for, whether you are normal or handicapped, the more your face and body reacts with a reciprocal glow of being wanted and esteemed as a person of worth. I think I was lucky that on Skylark even the children with the most contorted limbs, even the ones that constantly dribbled, sneezed and vomited, could still smile and react positively. I was lucky too in that some of the children had faces that were, by any standards, good to look at.

There now follow individual profiles of children typical of those in the group:

Chapter 3

PROFILES

JOHN (FOURTEEN YEARS)

Due to an over-precipitate delivery before the arrival of the midwife, John was concussed at birth resulting in quadriplegia – severe cerebral palsy affecting his whole body. His limbs were normally contracted, but he sometimes made uncontrolled movements of his legs and arms (athetoid movements), particularly when over-stimulated. He had a little voluntary control of his head and left arm, had good eyesight and hearing, smiled, laughed loudly, and had many facial expressions for different emotions. He made sounds as if attempting to speak.

John will always make me think of a captive bird, trying most of the time to reach the enticing world which he could glimpse through the bars of his cage. The cage was his body.

Because John had a tremendous desire to communicate he always formed a strong relationship with his teacher, looking to her to be his interpreter and link with the world. In the same way he was very co-operative most of the time with the other adults he had got to know well, and liked: his charge nurse, physiotherapist or nurses who came back after they had left the ward so that they could take him out for walks or expeditions. He was also very fond of his family.

John was wary when approached by friendly strangers and one of the first things I learnt about him was his immense range of facial expressions from beaming welcome and delight to looks as black as thunder. I also learnt not to allow him to manipulate me with these 'secret weapons'! He used his whole body to communicate. He could contract into a

9

tight ball of rejecting disapproval; when pleased he waved his arms and kicked his legs with a strong, rapid action. He had enormous variation of mood, partly depending on how he was feeling physically, and partly depending on the amount of adult attention he was, or was not receiving.

In every sense John was the brightest child in the group. The psychologists gave him a mental age of between two years four months and two years eight months. I found that he understood and enjoyed activities and stories that a normal four- to five-year-old does. John had an intense desire to learn, to please and to achieve. The tremendous problem he set his teacher was how to fulfil his classroom expectations.

Those who worked with him over a period of time suspected that he did speak, but his physical disability and lack of control of his mouth and neck muscles made it impossible for one to understand what his spoken words actually were. By using a tape recorder and playing his sounds back slowly, I was able to discern quite clearly 'Ann', 'Hello!', 'Yes'. I wanted to find a possible interpreter of his speech from among the verbal patients in the hospital. Unfortunately there was only one verbal child on John's ward and he attended a different class. Although he and John were quite friendly, and enjoyed being together out of school time, I could not get him to explain John's sounds to me. Possibly, if John were moved on to a ward where there are more verbal patients of higher intelligence, and if he managed to form a good relationship with one of them, he might find an interpreter as Joey did in his remarkable autobiography *Tongue-tied*.[1]

John had a real appreciation of what might be called the *naturally* good things of life. This ability to discriminate between the genuine article and the synthetic product he applied to people's feelings for him, to situations and to material objects. Regarding food, John found it very difficult to swallow or to chew. Unless he took tiny sips, or was given very small mouthfuls of soft food he choked, spluttered and coughed violently. But he loved cooking and good food. One

Christmas at our home there were egg and banana sandwiches, soft chocolate biscuits, jelly and mousse on the tea table, as well as a rich home-made hard-iced Christmas cake. To my surprise he ate a sandwich and biscuit without much enthusiasm. 'What would you like now John?' His face lit up, his arms waved obviously in the direction of the Christmas cake. We cut him a small piece and with real enjoyment he ate his way slowly through cake, marzipan and icing. 'What next John? Would you like some mousse?' A frown that said 'No!'. I suggested everything else on the table. No response. In desperation I asked if he wanted another piece of Christmas cake, beams of joy from John, who once again slowly and with great deliberation finished up every crumb.

In the same way John loved the natural world. From the classroom window we watched the birds arrive on our bird-table. John helped us keep a chart of the different species with the dates and times of arrival and departure. From his wheelchair he helped to re-stock the table with water, bread, nuts and bits of bacon rind. We looked up the birds in a bird book to identify the rarer species, and we listened with the other children to records of birdsongs.[2] On the grass just outside the ward we sat quietly and watched a water wagtail drink delicately from a puddle; crows, redwings and lapwings feeding; and often on warmer days we watched skylarks rising up high above the ward singing as they soared.

It was the same with wild flowers. John would love to be taken outside to help pick these by lying over a foam wedge. One spring we made a collection of as many as we could find within the hospital grounds and outside in the nearby lanes and hedges. We brought them all back into the classroom for the other children to see, feel and smell. Then we made a huge mural of fields and trees. We cut out flowers, birds and butterflies as like the originals as possible, with their names printed underneath. John and the other children helped to paste on the shapes. (See the chapter on Group Activities, page 75.)

John liked to be useful and to do purposeful activities such as helping to wash up and dry, to polish his shoes, dust tables and help with a long-handled broom to sweep the floor. He enjoyed any form of water play but he much preferred to use the water trough not just to play with water toys but to wash and wring out small garments. On these occasions we added a little soap liquid to the water and after he had, with help, washed the clothes we would put a bucket of clean water on the floor on his left side and he would gradually pick up the clothes and drop them into the bucket for rinsing. We then helped him to squeeze out the excess water and, with the damp garments on the tray of his wheelchair, we would hang them on a line to dry. John found it easier to fix the clothes on the line with the old-fashioned 'gypsy' pegs, rather than with the modern spring-clip variety. Once the clothes were dry we would set up an ironing board and he would help to iron and put them to air on a radiator. I was always thinking of John's future and hoped that some skill in simple activities would gain John a place in a verbal occupational therapy group once he was past school age. We did a great deal of pasting and cutting out with special scissors made by ESA.[3] With a little help he could cut card with a paper guillotine and bang with a paper punch or stapler, and he used to help us prepare all the cards our children sent home to their families at Christmas and Easter.

John loved to try to draw, write letters and paint but he disliked being helped all the time and it seemed impossible for him to hold a pencil in such a way that the tip made contact with the paper. Using sellotape we bound clip-clothes pegs as handles on to felt pens and paint brushes. Now, by tightly grasping the peg, John could bring the pen down at right angles on to the paper and 'draw' unaided. By using a plastic stencil alphabet we could now help him to write short letters home. He loved to address the envelope, lick it up, put the stamp on and then be taken to the village letter box to post it. His family responded marvellously by sending him many more letters and postcards. This led on to our making birthday books for all the children, into which they helped us stick all their cards and letters, and we gradually added photographs of themselves, their families and outings. Many of the children, besides John, loved to look at their books, and families sent more cards once they realised they were being kept and treasured in this way. One mother wrote to tell her son that she was keeping her own birthday book into which she was sticking the cards that he made and sent to her.

As John had a little more voluntary control of his left arm than of any other limb, we taught him to raise this arm as the answer 'yes' to our questions. It took him time and concentration to do this but it worked. As another form of communication we had a simple board made for him on which there were four shutters with large handles. Under each shutter we pasted various pictures such as a tea set, a television set, a country scene and a washing-up bowl. We could ask him to close all the shutters over the things he did not want to do and leave open the one he did. He demonstrated that he knew his colours by using the brightly coloured Play Pax cubes.[4] Whatever colour I asked for he would eventually manage to pick out of a large box, even if this took ten minutes.

The great love of John's life was bathing. In the water he had much more freedom of movement. He loved to splash vigorously with his legs while lying outside in a large paddling pool, or on our rare trips to the children's play park pools, or better still at the seaside. The construction of a hospital hydro-therapy pool will bring John and many of the other severely disabled children a real extension of life. I think he might learn to swim. He also loved riding, supported by three skilled helpers, when a group of Riding for the Disabled[5] started in the hospital.

John had very acute hearing and sight and an excellent memory and visual recall. From across a wide room he would hear discussion of a special treat that involved him. Immediately his feet would beat a tattoo, both arms would come up

13

and wave wildly in the air and a huge grin spread across his face. Mention of his forthcoming birthday, of bonfire night, preparations for Christmas or a walk to the shops, produced this immediate reaction. Once his mother told me about an incident on a family picnic, years before when John was living at home. John's face showed that he remembered the occasion well and he laughed delightedly at the bit where, by mistake, he had rolled, on his own, right the way down a long grassy bank. Once he knew my own children he would love to listen to simple anecdotes about how naughty or lazy they had been the day before at home. He enjoyed simple stories about domestic events read from books, and the radio and television programmes for pre-school children. Stories from 'Listen with Mother' (BBC) on records gave him great pleasure, provided an adult was near at hand to keep his attention focused.

John will probably never be able to feed or dress himself. I felt that given enough nursing time he might eventually be toilet trained. He certainly loved to choose his own clothes on shopping expeditions and to sit in the front of a long mirror to admire new clothes and shoes. He liked to help brush his hair and wash his face and took great pride in looking neat and smart.

John's future life will develop happily provided that those who know and grow to love him will continually seek to find new ways through which he can communicate his wants and his feelings to those of us outside.

HILDA (TEN YEARS)

Hilda suffered cyanosis at birth (some oxygen starvation) resulting from a protracted and difficult labour. She was quadriplegic but with voluntary control of her head. Her legs were stiff and contracted, and she was prone to very violent startle reflex actions and severe spasm of chest muscles. She had good eyesight and hearing, smiled, laughed loudly and had many facial expressions for different emotions. She used a few distinct words to attract adult attention.

Hilda was one of those remarkable severely handicapped and subnormal children, who had the most normal, beautiful face. When she smiled and laughed she lit up into a picture of radiant health and happiness. She had long, glistening dark brown hair, great brown eyes that followed with alert attention all that went on around her, and a soft golden complexion and skin that acquired 'a glorious sun tan' as soon as she went outside for the first warm spring or summer day.

Hilda had a great sense of mischievous fun. She was fascinated by voice intonation and was keenly aware if, for instance, two members of staff stood near her having a confidential or gossipy conversation, she would turn her head to listen to each speaker in turn as if she relished every word they were saying, and if one broke off to say: 'Now, Hilda, not a word to anyone, remember!', she would throw back her head with a shout of laughter. Hilda also loved minor disasters which involved the discomfiture of an adult, and this was a child whose mental level was assessed to be similar to that of a one-year-old!

On the first day I took charge of the class I was extremely nervous of my new responsibilities and decided – rashly – to organise a water play session. This involved several trips to the sluice to collect buckets of warm water with which to fill the trough. Just as I staggered back into the room with my third bucketful, the charge nurse appeared from his office, saying 'the Head on the phone for you!' Startled, I turned, slipped and spilt water everywhere, liberally sprinkling Hilda who was sitting in a sag bag. She jumped and gave a tremendous shout of joy at my obvious muddle!

Someone running through the room, elderly ladies on bicycles in the village, someone up a step ladder cleaning windows or hanging Christmas decorations, all evoked the same laughter. She revelled in the bizarre, the unexpected, the humorous.

Hilda's highly developed social sense – she greeted every

15

newcomer with shouts of 'Hello! Hello! Hello!' – and her fluid distractability, meant she had to be taken out to a quiet room, or surrounded by screens in order to get her co-operation with physiotherapy or a specific learning task. On a really 'naughty' day she would even shout 'Hello!' at the feet that she heard passing. Her spasticity gave her whole body a tremendous backward thrust and she could become completely rigid all over with her rib cage gigantically distended. This made it difficult for her to breathe and she would quickly panic, break out in a sweat and become very distressed. Too much excitement increased this rigidity. To counteract this harmful sequence we worked under the physiotherapist's guidance to break the backward thrust by getting her firmly into a supported sitting position on the floor or in a low chair. We would gradually bend her spine forwards with her arms out in front of her. Then with firm handling and soothing conversation we got her to relax her body and arms and slowly her hands would become a little more flexible. To encourage her to hold this position we would put a paint brush in her hand and help her to paint on a table easel, or help her to do a simple inset puzzle which had large knobs that she could grasp on each piece.

In four years Hilda advanced from lying rigid on the floor, screaming in protest, when approached by a physiotherapist, to being able to sit reasonably well in a padded wheelchair or in an ordinary low chair with her feet on a wedge, and a table tucked well into her waist. In this position she sometimes played at the sand or water troughs, used the play equipment or watched a fifteen-minute children's programme like 'You and me' or 'Play school'. It also meant she was able to take part in our other sitting group activities (see chapter 7).

Hilda could be very temperamental and difficult (especially with new members of staff), stiffening and spitting out food and drinks. When she did this we would take her away to a far corner of the room and tell her she could not come back until she had finished screaming. She responded very well to this kind of decisive discipline and would soon roll over with a big smile that said 'I'm sorry'.

As a young child at home Hilda had acquired the clear enunciation of a few key words, but no one seemed able to extend this range, apart from 'Oh dear!' and 'good girl', which seemed to develop during the years I was teaching her.

Hilda was an immensely warm, affectionate child who made lasting relationships with the members of staff who took a particular interest in her and remained long enough on the ward for such a relationship to develop. This seemed to reflect the love that the whole of her very large, extended family showed towards her and towards each other. She had always been a much-loved child and this seemed to glow from her. Her family lived over forty miles away in a remote rural area but scarcely a weekend passed without someone visiting her. Her family would have loved to have kept her at home but she needed daily physiotherapy and classroom teaching. Most parents of a child on Skylark Ward had found that the constant lifting of a heavy, awkward, totally dependent, doubly incontinent child, who could do virtually nothing for itself, was an impossible burden, especially as they nearly all had normal children as well.

ANGELA (SIX YEARS)

Angela was the surviving twin (the other being still-born) from a premature birth. She suffered severe cerebral palsy with athetoid movements. She had no vision, very little hearing, and was subject to frequent epileptic fits.

Angela was one of the most profoundly handicapped children on the ward. She constantly regurgitated food and drink and was subject to severe chest infections. Her IQ was assessed as equivalent to that of a three-month-old normal baby. But Angela could move around. Despite being very floppy and having little control of her head or limbs she had taught herself to rise from a lying to a sitting position. Gradually, with the help of the physiotherapists, she

17

acquired better head control and longer periods of sitting upright. As she moved around more the physiotherapist made her a padded helmet using a red plastic baseball cap such as children wore on a nearby US airforce base. Now when Angela moved off the mat she could flop over without hurting her head.

Angela had a dear little face and we discovered that she loved to lie with the sunshine full on it. Maybe she *could* discriminate between total light and darkness. She seemed to enjoy sitting on our laps and having her hands moved about in warm water and freely flowing silver sand. We found that her writhing body would quieten and a look of peace come over her face when we held her close to loud music. Something really powerful like a recording of Beethoven's 'Emperor Concerto' lulled her into what seemed like a mood of contentment. Her family had also noticed this when she was at home.

At times she liked to be nursed and cuddled and to have her cheeks delicately caressed with a feather or fingertips. At other times she indicated that she wanted to be free to move about on the mat alone. She seemed to practise, conscientiously, her sitting position and the physiotherapist confirmed a steady development in the strength of her head and shoulder muscles. It seemed amazing that a child so cut off from the usual sources of stimulation and encouragement still had this drive to learn and to improve.

We had several children who made themselves sick by sticking their fingers down their throats. Having decided that this was probably a habit engendered by boredom we let them have more freedom of movement on the mat. Sometimes one had to mop up quickly, but it seemed that the children were less sick than when they were strapped in their wheelchairs. Being bored surely showed some kind of potential?

Angela had a devoted family with two delightful younger brothers who made themselves completely at home whenever they visited the ward or the classroom. Angela went home for the school holidays and seemed most peaceful and happy when her family visited her. She always looked more 'normal' once they gathered round her.

A most touching relationship developed between Angela and Ben, one of the ward domestics. This young lad of eighteen really loved Angela. He had no family of his own and lived in 'digs'. From his wages he bought special clothes and toys for Angela, including a little pair of red-striped dungarees and matching sun hat for our trips to the seaside. When he was not on duty Ben would make special trips into the hospital to see Angela, and would often feed her as a voluntary job in addition to his domestic work.

Because of his love for Angela and the other Skylark children Ben gave up the better wages of a domestic to become a nursing auxiliary and so spend more time with the children. He then began to study for some exams in the hope that he might eventually enrol for the pupil nurse training. Dismissed by some as loud-mouthed, unsuitably dressed, with a bit of a reputation for getting involved in pub fights when off duty, Ben knew more about what makes a handicapped child 'tick' than many a so-called professional.

There were, in fact, a number of young people around the hospital, classed by some as 'troublemakers', who found a deep satisfaction in helping those who were more disadvantaged than themselves. They seemed to have a natural empathy with the profoundly handicapped that many others might envy.

I began to realise what others are proving in various new experiments in living,[6] that some unhappy men and women find a new direction by working with mentally handicapped children and adults. As well as the 'Bens' of this life, several highly educated, intelligent, young men and women found that Skylark Ward acted as a catalyst. These were people who after one or two years at university had become disillusioned with what they called 'the academic rat-race' and the glittering prizes society was meant to have in store for them. For various reasons they dropped out of academic life and they dropped into Skylark, more by luck than judgment, as untrained, low paid, overworked nursing auxiliaries.

They were always in the classroom asking questions about the children and finding their own ways of encouraging them. After a year, two decided to go back to university but to read a totally different subject. A brilliant ex-scholar left us to visit India. On his return he got a place at a London hospital in order to study for the State Registered Nurse qualification and then to do psychiatric nurse training. Another began a training as an occupational therapist. All agreed that the breathing space they had on Skylark had helped them. In a curious way it all seemed to add up, both for them and for the children.

PAMELA (FOUR YEARS)

The cause of Pamela's brain damage was not established. She suffered severe cerebral palsy affecting her body from the waist downwards, but had good voluntary control of her arms and head. Her eyesight and hearing were good. She would smile and chuckle, and make noises typical of a normal six-month-old baby. She cried when lonely and in pain.

Pamela was the child in the group who evoked my strongest maternal feelings. I suppose she was the one I most wanted to 'mother'. She was a small, very appealing little child. People in charge of a group of children, whether they are their own or on loan from other people, can never allow themselves 'a favourite', and all the children in the group obviously had their different ways of eliciting love and had different needs which we tried to meet. But it would be dishonest not to acknowledge that given the opportunity I would have gathered her up and taken her home for good!

Looking back, I think she had this effect on me partly because, unlike the rest of the children in the group, she came into the hospital after I had been there for two years, and was an exceptionally young child for permanent residential care, straight from a very caring home life. All the

20

other children had been in the group and in the hospital for several years. Pamela was my only 'home' child and I hated the fact that she had to leave it. Like Hilda, her capacity to respond lovingly had not been damaged by the making and breaking of meaningful relationships, nor by a constant shift from one foster home to another before arriving with us. I felt too that her behaviour showed her bewilderment. She cried a very great deal when she first came in and was only comforted by being nursed. She used a number of attention-seeking devices.

She was also a very affectionate little girl. She would lean forward and stroke one's cheeks, smiling and making a long sustained 'ah, ah, ah' sound of pleasure. She was very pretty. Her face was finely modelled with high cheek bones. She had soft curly brown hair, bright grey eyes, and the most beautiful child's hands I have ever seen, with long slender fingers. She was, in fact able to do more with them than any other child in the group. She learned quickly to give herself her own drink from a double-handled mug and to strike a chime bar during music sessions without any help.

Probably because of her recent home setting she seemed much more aware of the other children and enjoyed doing things with them. She loved to sit on one side of a low table with another small child opposite her, and, between them, a large sheet of paper liberally sprinkled with dollops of thick coloured paint. She and her partner would produce masterpieces of palm and finger painting. I have one framed in my study and look at it while I am writing this.

Pamela was unable to sit up on her own but she had developed considerable strength in her small, slender arms and had a very strong downward pull. The physiotherapist wanted us to encourage her to use her arms to pull herself up into a sitting position. Over the very large mat in the centre of the classroom we hung plastic garden netting and from this dangled things like chains, balls, bells and rattles. Pamela loved to grasp a red hoop-la hoop and tug it up and down until the whole net tinkled and clashed. This pleased Pamela and delighted the other immobile children who had not the strength to create such an uproar. Sometimes we would sit Pamela, strapped in a special small chair, beside a hospital trolley from which we suspended at varying heights a collection of kitchen equipment. Again with a partner opposite her, she would orchestrate wooden spoons, small saucepans, a colander, a metal pepper pot, an egg whisk and saucepan lids. This kind of occupation kept Pamela in a good remedial position – backbone straightened, hips and knees in line, feet flat on the floor. She was extending the range and strength of her grasp, getting tactile, aural and visual stimulation, encouraging a less able child to do the same, and, most important of all, having a good time!

Pamela needed constant changes of position, otherwise she stiffened from the waist downwards and it hurt. When this happened she liked to lie on her tummy right across one's lap with toys on the floor which she could play with.

I loved to. watch her face light up when her family came to visit her. She was particularly fond of her older sister and little two-year-old brother, who were both normal, very intelligent, good-looking children. Pamela would sit on her mother's lap and stroke her little brother's hair. When a family with young siblings visited during school time we would sometimes set out small tables with a dolls' tea set, little biscuits and milk in the jugs. A few other children, like John and Hilda, would love to join such a circle and have a pretend tea party, eating and helping to pour out the milk.

The fact that Pamela left a loving home for a permanent life in an institution, illustrates most clearly the strain that a very handicapped child exerts on a mother who is loving, intelligent, highly strung, unsupported by an extended family and fully cognisant of what the future holds for such a child. It seems to be a question of the individual mother's 'level of tolerance', and this is partly decided by the amount, or lack of support she receives in carrying the burden of her children.

There are several written accounts by mothers like

22

Pamela's, women whose life is a continual 'running sore' because of their anguish, remorse and guilt at being unable to cope with the demands of their normal children plus the added burden of one who is profoundly handicapped.[7]

It seems that a woman can be torn to pieces by her own expectations of herself as a wife and mother. Such women cannot equate the demands made upon them by husband, normal children and a handicapped child. The complexity of demands she places upon herself is beyond fulfilment. Sometimes the situation is made harder for her because her husband feels differently about the handicapped child, and only feels capable of being a good father to his normal children.

Perhaps it is also a question of the age spacing of the children. Where the handicapped child comes last, or in the middle of a large family, the parents may be strongly supported by their normal children who willingly share the burden of cherishing their handicapped sibling and strongly resist residential care for their brother or sister. This kind of family support has also been recorded by heroic parents.[8]

Each family situation is unique. Family feelings must be respected. Those who manage to 'carry' a profoundly handicapped child win our admiration. Those who cannot and pass their child into permanent residential care should win our sympathy and respect for the honesty of a decision that is probably rarely without lingering remorse.

If, in the near future, our society could provide more family support units, as described on page 108 we might be able to spare families like Pamela's, Hilda's and John's, and many others, the searing all-or-nothing decision between total home care or total institutional care for a handicapped child.

ROBERT (NINE YEARS)

Robert was one of undiagnosed twins – the other one born first being normal. He had severe cerebral palsy with little

23

voluntary control of his head and neck. He ate and drank with difficulty. He could crawl in a primitive fashion on his stomach, and made wild, unco-ordinated arm movements. He had some impairment of vision, but good hearing; he would smile and laugh, and cry when distressed.

Robert had the most extraordinary response to sound. He was quite clearly 'turned on' by certain noises and deeply disturbed by others. He came from a musical family and he loved instrumental music provided it was not too loud and overwhelming. He paid little attention to music on records or on the television. He disliked the piano accordion which made him weep, but he adored the guitar and the piano, and, to a lesser extent, the harp, the recorder and the flute. He also loved 'funny noises'. The sudden scrape of a chair leg, the sound of a wound-up mechanical toy, adults making animal noises, all had him in fits of giggles.

He was a slight child with Latin good looks – sleek dark hair, a dusky skin and dark eyes. He always had a look of joyful anticipation as we set out the toys. He moved about with a seal-like action and was very curious, often going on journeys of exploration, usually towards the source of an unusual sound or a brightly coloured toy. If someone sat on the mat and played the guitar he was there in no time so that he could twang the strings with his characteristic claw-like action. Like Pamela he had a good strong downward pull with his arms. Together they sometimes sat in a tractor tyre under a hospital trolley which was fitted with a light and pull-on switch. We varied the colour of the light bulb, and sometimes made a tent with cloths of different colours so that they sat inside together pulling the light on and off.

It is possible that this play gradually taught both of them something about causal connexions. Certainly everyone, including the physiotherapist, was very surprised that when they were both given new, freer-wheeling chairs, they both learnt, very quickly, to propel themselves around the room towards any object or activity that interested them.

It was very difficult to get Robert to look people straight in the eye. He had, as far as we knew, reasonably good eyesight, but for some reason he would give only the most fleeting, almost accidental, glances. He seemed to make a deliberate effort to avoid looking into people's eyes. We used to wonder whether this resistance was in some way linked with the fact that he had spent the first year of life in an institution where, like all the other babies, he had had the minimum amount of handling by his caretakers, and probably no encouragement to relate warmly to a single person or to play. Maybe he had spent that vital first year seeing little except his cot, white walls and a white ceiling.

For ages we worked very hard to encourage him to look us in the eye, but with little success. It was during my last months with the group that we began to have a series of breakthroughs. It all began one morning when I was alone with him in the quiet room. I laid him on his back on a large rubber inflatable and standing over him I rested both his feet up against my thighs. I held his hands in mine and called his name. He looked up and straight into my eyes and sustained his gaze for longer than ever before. He then turned his head and looked at a toy beside him, and then he turned and looked back at me. He did this three times before turning his head firmly away and obviously switching off contact. When I tried the same technique the next day it did not work but a week later it did. From then onwards he began to look at us briefly from other positions, as if he could at last tolerate, at least briefly, real contact with another human being. His expression gradually acquired more vitality.

Robert also found it very difficult to concentrate on the toy or materials he was playing with – what we called 'making eye–hand co-ordination'. He tended to make swipes at toys while looking over his shoulder at something else. Many of his hand and arm movements were wild and rather mean-ingless. He loved the feel of sand and water, but left to himself he just scooped up enormous quantities out of the troughs and flung them on the floor. We used to hold one arm to encourage him to make better use of the other one.

We were lucky enough to have a student volunteer, Geoffrey, who gradually built up a very good relationship with Robert. Geoffrey would take Robert into the quiet room and work through single activities like posting shapes through the Kiddicraft post box.

We were trying to get Robert to sit without support, so Geoffrey would sit on the floor opposite Robert, with his long legs acting as side supports, and with gentle, low whistles bring Robert's attention back to the task in hand when his eyes and hands wandered. Week after week, patiently and consistently, Geoffrey worked with Robert and strengthened their relationship by looking after Robert on outings, taking him out of doors to play on the grass, taking him for walks in a push-chair and sitting him on his lap during sessions with the music therapist.

Geoffrey studied the individual programme of aims (see pages 35–36) and equipment that we had worked out as suitable for Robert; he watched the physiotherapists working with him (see page 36); and then he used his own initiative when working with Robert to think up new ways in which to reinforce what we and the physiotherapists were trying to achieve. This concerted approach showed results in Robert's progress and it also had an important influence on Geoffrey himself.

Geoffrey, who had already brought volunteers into other wards of the hospital, now brought several of his student friends to Skylark. All these young people had the same mature appreciation of what we were trying to achieve with the children. Each one of them took over a particular child and worked as Geoffrey did with Robert. Geoffrey himself had been destined for a career in the law, but, having taken his first degree, decided to 'take a break' and work as a ward orderly in another hospital. The next we heard was that Geoffrey, now twenty-three, had been appointed organiser of a new national organisation for handicapped people. I am sure Geoffrey will achieve much in this field. He still visits Robert, who has, I suppose, helped to change the direction of

Geoffrey's thought and life – and perhaps through him many other lives as well.

HENRY (TEN YEARS)

The cause of Henry's brain damage was not established. He had severe cerebral palsy affecting his legs and feet, but good voluntary control of head and arms. He had some impairment of vision and hearing, and made sounds as a means of communication, but no identifiable words. At times he was very withdrawn and cried a great deal. He smiled and laughed. He suffered severe bouts of epileptic fits.

I found Henry the most perplexing child in the group. As with Pamela I wanted very much to 'mother' him. He was again a very good-looking child, small, inclined to be plump, with fair hair, bright rosy cheeks, pale blue eyes and an entrancing smile. Henry could sit very well, quite unsupported, and with an adult holding both hands he could walk with a very stiff, hesitant gait. Sadly, the spasticity in his feet and legs grew steadily worse despite constant physiotherapy, and it was considered unlikely that he would ever walk on his own.

He was a very strange little boy and probably had autistic tendencies. He responded immediately to attention with smiles and giggles of delight, but one felt this was an almost automatic reflex and had little real significance. Sometimes, for no diagnosed reasons, he would have weeks of constant bitter crying and great distress. At such times the tears poured down his cheeks and he was inconsolable even when nursed, rocked, hugged, carried about, or alternatively left to cry on his own. He also went through periods of frequent epileptic fits and then months when he had no apparent fit at all.

He was one of the most fundamentally withdrawn children in the group although this was covered by a façade of social cheerfulness. I felt he was in a world of his own most of the time, and when he cried it was a very dark frightening world

27

in which to be alone. It was very difficult to get him to take any interest in his surroundings. Left to himself he rocked violently to and fro and held both hands to his mouth. For a long time I could not get him to reach out for any toy. Suddenly one day, while sitting with other children round the water tray, he began quite spontaneously to splash both hands furiously in the water making high-pitched shrieks. He got wilder and wilder with his splashing, water went everywhere, but gradually he grew calmer and the shrieking subsided. From that time on he always enjoyed water play, sometimes just using one hand with the other at his mouth, sometimes using both hands for brief spells. After this he began to play more freely with the sand but we had to fit a wide polystyrene 'ruff' round his neck so that he did not swallow too much sand every time his hands went back to his mouth.

Now when Henry sat at a table with toys in front of him his attitude was ambivalent. He seemed to want to reach for them, especially toys like the Escor swings and roundabouts, but he seemed afraid to take his hands away from his mouth. Occasionally he seemed to pluck up enough courage, or initiative, to make a quick grabbing movement which often knocked the toy flying. Just before my last Christmas with the group we were all busy making a crib scene. There was a plastic bag filled with straw on the table. Suddenly Henry leant forward and started to make a succession of furtive grabs at the bag. He began to laugh at the scrunching noise of the straw inside. We stood quietly and he spent an hour playing more and more freely with the bag until there was straw everywhere, all over Henry, the table and the floor.

We made Henry a low trolley on free-wheeling castors and he used to move himself about a little using his hands to keep his balance. I felt he needed some kind of special 'baby walker' in which to explore the room for himself and thus distract his hands away from his mouth. In the Princess Marina Hospital, Northampton, I saw children in 'lobster pot walkers' specially designed there to give children like

Henry more mobility. These consisted of a thick rubber band round the children's waist, or under the armpits, with metal legs and free-running castors. I could visualise Henry using his hands to steady himself and gradually exploring his surroundings. When I left the group a walker was on order for Henry and two other children.

BERNARD (SEVENTEEN YEARS)

During pregnancy, Bernard's mother was involved in a road accident, and the birth was a difficult forceps delivery. Bernard had a very curved spine and severe cerebral palsy, particularly affecting the left side of his body (hemiplegia). He had very poor vision and some hearing. He suffered severe epileptic fits. He would smile and laugh, and cry when lonely.

Bernard was the oldest child in the school group. It was local policy to allow children to remain on the school register until eighteen plus, if there was evidence that they were still gaining something from an educational programme. When people think of a special care unit they often visualise a number of extremely handicapped, large, immobile, non-reacting children, lying about on a mat. Sometimes the heart sinks. What *can* we do to educate these children? Superficially, Bernard was one such child.

Bernard was very large and heavy (it took three women to lift him) and he shrieked a lot of the time, a high-pitched, ear-splitting scream. He was the only child in the group whose family had apparently lost all contact with him. Officially he would be described as 'abandoned'. He dribbled and sneezed constantly, and he was often sick after food and drinks. Bernard was certainly hard work. But Bernard was a human being like you and me; he had his own special needs and some talents. He could use his right hand a little.

After a time we realised he often screamed because he was hungry, uncomfortable or wanted attention. Because he had a large appetite the charge nurse allowed us to feed him with

29

small sandwiches between meals, and he learnt gradually to use his right hand to feed these to himself. If we changed his position several times a session he was much happier. He liked to get the weight off his spine by lying on his stomach across a sag bag or on an inflatable. He also liked to lie with a companion on a very simple seesaw made from a large door placed on two triangular shaped pieces of wood, covered by a soft mattress. Bernard and friends loved to be seesawed gently up and down to the rhythm of 'See Saw, Marjorie Daw'. Sometimes we hoisted him into a huge hospital pram which, detached from its wheels, was hung by ropes from a hefty government supply coat stand. Propped with pillows, and swinging gently to and fro, Bernard felt more part of the scene. By hanging large bells, bright plastic lanterns, Chinese tinkle bars and other mobiles from the stand, we got Bernard and other poorly sighted children to 'track with their eyes' by looking upwards. Some seemed to see better at this angle than at any other.

Bernard loved to lie on a mattress with his good arm and hand over the edge of a tray of water or sand and dabble the contents about. We also found that, wedged with cushions in an ordinary chair in front of a standing easel, he enjoyed being helped to paint, and if we tilted the finished picture about at various angles near his face Bernard made an effort to see and admire his handiwork. He liked to touch the other children. He also liked pulling a pillow over his face with his right arm and he enjoyed the sound of his fingers scratching the plastic mat on which he sometimes lay. Left alone for long Bernard would burst into loud exaggerated sobs rather like a disgruntled normal toddler. When pleased, Bernard laughed a lot.

It seemed to us that multiply handicapped children *do* smile and laugh a great deal. Their sense of humour is often developed well beyond their other qualities, certainly far beyond their psychologically assessed mental ages. Not inane, pointless laughter but sometimes something quite sophisticated. What makes them laugh varies with the child.

All of ours laughed when tickled. Robert laughed at unexpected noises; Hilda and several others loved slapstick comedy. John had a well-developed sense of the ridiculous. Sometimes they laughed at each other's misfortunes as well as at our simulated or actual 'muddles'. They laughed when singing; music and dancing made them feel gay. Most smiled or laughed when an adult paused to speak to them. They laughed when we joked among ourselves. Handicapped children can feel sad, bored, neglected, rejected, physically uncomfortable, frightened, but given adequate attention and stimulation a special care unit can be a place of laughter and happiness, in which adults and children can forget for a while the problems and griefs of their private worlds.

Bernard was growing gradually 'more alive'. Everyone who knew him noticed this. He began to use his hands to play with toys more often and for longer periods. He sat up more to see what was going on. He may continue to develop slowly for many years, because very slow learners can go on learning for a long time. Bernard and the other children taught us never to say 'Oh! he'll never do so and so', because the very next day he may do it for the first time ever, and your heart will turn over in the way it does when your child quickens in the womb, or your normal one-year-old suddenly takes his first few tottering steps.

ANNE (FIVE YEARS)

Anne was paraplegic but with voluntary control of arms and head. She had some impairment of vision, good hearing and made some attempt to use identifiable words. She would smile, laugh and make noises typical of a normal nine-month-old baby.

I think of Anne whenever I pass the city cemetery. It is a very large, very ordinary graveyard with few trees and regular paths forming a massive grid. On its northern boundary there is still space for more graves, and beyond the high green railings and straggling bushes stretch flat ploughed fields.

One morning in early spring, in a fog so enveloping that the only sounds were of dripping water, and the damp cold seeped into one's bones, a group of six people stood with teeth clenched against chattering under a single silver birch tree. Anne's tiny pale wood coffin decked with home-made bunches of daffodils and primroses was lowered into the earth and the little party made its several ways home. A clergyman, one relative, a social worker, Anne's headmistress, her physiotherapist and her teacher left the cemetery with many conflicting thoughts.

Anne died on her fifth birthday. Her body was smaller than that of an emaciated one-year-old but her spirit was tremendous. She was lion-hearted. Despite her manifold handicaps she had a gusto for living only extinguished by her final, brief illness. Her legs were so stiff and contracted that she could sit only when propped up by cushions, but she could roll a little when flat on her back and use her arms and hands to reach for toys.

Her tiny face remains graven in my memory. She had a most appealing, impudent grin – and she was always smiling or chuckling – her teeth were crooked, her beady blue eyes squinted at you from under a wiry mop. She never showed any sign of self-pity: no complaining, whining or crying. One felt that if she had ever acquired speech it would have been witty and sardonic. It seems impossible that such a tiny malformed being could contain so much vivid spirit, so much sheer determination to survive and to improve. She loved to be tickled and romped with. She crowed with delight when nurses tossed her in the air and used her as a ball. She would pat their faces as if to ask for more.

During the few months she was with us she learnt to play a chime bar and beat on a drum during the music sessions. A little longer and she might have learnt to beat unaided and with exact timing. We used to lay her inside a large blown-up inner tube of a car wheel so that she would learn to stretch and straighten her legs and body, and develop her head control. We would put toys within her reach and she enjoyed

32

having another child opposite her, perhaps also lying extended over a foam rubber wedge, so that they could play together. Within the limits of her handicaps she was always 'on the go'. She particularly loved toys that clicked, rattled or rang bells when pulled by a string and she could shake rattles and bells. For a change of position we would lay Anne on her back with a variety of objects strung out above her so that she was encouraged to stretch up and to roll from side to side in order to explore the coloured, noisy toys overhead, and to extend her vision in varying directions.

Anne would sit on people's laps to reach into the sand and water troughs. In the summer out of doors I remember her in a tiny pair of blue and white dungarees and a round dark blue linen sun hat. She loved to lie in the paddling pool wriggling her body in the water and splattering the other children with her starfish hands. She was always the first to crow her greeting when I arrived on the ward in the morning. Because she was making such progress in movement and even beginning to say a few distinct words, and because she had become, in a sense, 'the life and soul of the party', her death came as a tremendous blow to everyone on the ward. She caught a massive infection and died in a few hours. We were all totally unprepared for her going and the influence of her personality was reflected in the shattering sense of loss we all felt. As a very young nursing assistant said, 'We could spare Anne least of all'.

The death of any child is a special tragedy. The death of a very handicapped one is obviously a release from perhaps years of increasing discomfort, pain and frustration. With extensive, costly surgery Anne might eventually have sat unsupported, but probably never walked. It would be unrealistic to want a child like Anne to live just because she had made progress and would have always enlivened the group she lived with. And yet her brief life had significance for all who knew her. One cannot remember Anne and indulge in a bout of self-pity.

33

Chapter 4

CHILD-BASED PROGRAMMES

When I took over the Skylark school group I was very fortunate in that I had worked as a volunteer for several months under its previous teacher. This meant that the children already knew me a little, and I had begun to make a good relationship with John (see page 9). The teacher, Harriet, had worked out an individual programme for each child in order to determine, as far as possible, its developmental level. She used the Piagetian stages of Sensori-Motor and (when applicable) Pre-Operational development and other good outlines based on the stages of a normal baby's development.[1] Harriet encouraged me, as a volunteer, to concentrate on working with one child at a time using her programme as a guideline. She also gave me ample opportunity to discuss each child with her during the lunch break. This convinced me of two things: the importance of supporting any voluntary helper at his appropriate level of interest, and the significance of a clear-cut programme for each child based on careful observation and continual review.

After I had been in charge for several months, and learnt more about the children from my own observation (see page 37) and from the whole team working with them: nursing staff, psychologists and physiotherapists (see page 43), I extended their individual programmes and began to work on some group activities and programmes (see page 68).

To illustrate the process of individual assessment, here is the programme I gradually evolved for Robert, our 'musical boy' (see his profile, page 23). I worked out a similar programme for each child.

34

Has extremely sensitive hearing and gets much delight from aural stimulation, provided it is not too loud.

Has good eyesight but needs help to focus on specific objects.

Reacts delightedly to interaction with other children and with adults; loves to be tickled.

Touches and fiddles with toys, especially if they make a noise.

Will crawl on his stomach in a primitive fashion towards objects that attract his attention, at times right across the room. In this way explores his surroundings spontaneously. (Unfortunately, this ability and natural curiosity has to be 'rationed' as it encourages a bad physical posture for Robert, contrary to physiotherapist aims for him, and is counter-productive by discouraging a good sitting and, perhaps, eventual standing position for him.)

In his wheelchair can move himself slowly around room to explore.

Will reach out for toys hanging in front, or slightly above him, especially if they produce a noise. Can pull light switch on and off.

Lies on back on an inflatable and will stretch out for toys within reach.

Sits quite well in ordinary chair up to low table with feet resting on a foam wedge – but not for longer than twenty minutes or may slide out of chair downwards.

In this position can use both hands and arms to play with things, which must be clamped or tied to the table or he will immediately sweep them on to the floor out of his reach.

Enjoys a wide range of play materials that give aural and tactile sensations. Shows no marked colour discrimination or preferences.

SUITABLE ACTIVITIES

Music, plucking guitar strings, rolling a musical ball; with adult help, hitting a chime bar or glockenspiel, shaking maraca, etc.

Painting. Unaided with hands. Needs help to hold brush, sponge, string. Put on plastic overall, secure paper very firmly to table or easel. Try to discourage claw-like unnatural action of hands.

Water Play. As Robert likes using wild, sweeping arm movements, put large plastic overall on him. Tie alternate hands to arm of chair for short periods in order to encourage more natural movement of the 'free' hand. Encourage him to use toys in the water and to touch the other children's hands.

Sand Play. As for water play. Robert also needs to wear a protective 'ruff' otherwise he swallows sand in large quantities.

Encourage handling of different textiles to develop tactile awareness and discrimination.

Work with Robert in a good sitting position, at a table or side-sitting with back support on the floor, or inside a rubber tyre. Work at times away from the group to encourage concentration and hand–eye co-ordination. Try to get eye contact.

Use long mirror to get him to look at himself while you adjust clothes, put on coat, shoes, socks. Brush and comb his hair, wash his face and brush his teeth. Get him to help you in very small ways.

Sit him on your lap, facing you, and play 'body games' like 'Round about the garden', or 'This little piggy went to market' with his bare toes. Sing to him, especially rocking lullabies.

He likes to sit up to the piano, on his own or with another child, and strike the keys. For this to be purposeful, work with him to develop a more natural action of hands and fingers; discourage his tendency to hit keys with clenched fists.

GENERAL AIMS

To work with physiotherapists at improving Robert's sitting position, in a small chair, with some support on a low stool or on the floor.

To improve Robert's hand–eye co-ordination by doing simple manipulative tasks with him.

Use your voice to get him to look into your eyes.

Encourage him to focus his eyes on any musical instrument you are helping him to play.

Prevent, as far as possible, unco-ordinated, purposeless use of his hands and arms with toys, water, sand, paint, etc. Curb his tendency to explore only partially a piece of apparatus by helping him to complete the task.

Always sit him up very straight before giving him food or drinks. Inhibit the backward thrust of his head (see self-help drinking programme, page 65).

SPECIAL APPARATUS FOR USE

Posting box, pyramid rings, books that make an animal noise when he helps to turn the pages.

Short television programmes during which you encourage him to look at the screen.

A record player that he can watch while listening to music, bird songs, animal noises.

Toys he can push and pull and that make a noise.

36

On Robert's arrival in Skylark, aged about three, he had apparently been a tiny, stiff, unresponsive child who screamed for hours with a weird, howling cry. Looking back, Robert made striking improvement at several levels during the five years I knew him. Physically he developed more control over his body, with a good prognosis of sitting eventually without support, and possibly standing in a suitable 'walker'. He was curious and could move about in his wheelchair to explore. He was now physically quite sturdy and had outgrown his earlier frequent attacks of asthma and severe respiratory infections. He could use his hands a little, and he could interact with toys if not actually 'play' with them. He looked alert, responsive and cheerful.

In his own way, Robert was a 'success story'. His improvement seemed largely due to constant physiotherapy linked with his school programme, his striking response to sound and music, and his attraction to a particular music therapist. He was luckier than many other Skylark children because of this innate enjoyment of music; also he had started regular physiotherapy earlier in life than many of the other children.

He will always be a severely spastic person totally dependent on adults for feeding, dressing and changing, but he has more opportunities for enjoying life than many of the other children because his curiosity, and social and musical response, will always win for him a fair degree of adult attention and interaction.

OBSERVING AND REACTING

Robert's story illustrates the overwhelming importance of minute observation in looking after profoundly handicapped children. Coupled with this constant scrutiny is the need to react sensitively to all the clues that daily searching and imaginative observation can yield. Against this background of information about the child one can then begin to set up a series of goals for him, a series of tiny steps forward.

37

Dr Albert Kushlick has totally altered the pattern of care for multiply handicapped people in the Wessex Region around Southampton, England by setting up a series of hostels for them, located in a community setting. The document that has attempted to evaluate this new pattern of care is worth detailed examination.[2] He dismisses as 'fuzzies' such vague phrases as 're-inforcing a person's sense of Identity' and replaces these by actual observable 'performances' like 'hold his coat and guide his hand to the armhole'. 'It is important to identify the tasks which the performers are to carry out in terms which are clear or allow minimal ambiguity. Tasks written in performance terms as distinct from "fuzzies" have this quality.'

From my own limited experience it seems to be essential that one must *know* the handicapped child before one can begin to *do* anything effectively. All people working with profoundly handicapped must consciously, and persistently, sharpen their powers of observation, imaginative perception and loving reaction or interaction with them.

The more handicapped the child and the fewer his normal channels of communication, the greater this challenge of acute observation becomes. The person handling the profoundly handicapped child must watch for every shred of evidence the child may give about his feelings and his understanding. The adult must make a sustained effort to imagine, all the time, what the world may look like through the eyes of *this* child, what it sounds like, what it feels like. It is an almost impossible task to even begin to imagine what it feels like to be severely mentally handicapped and physically handicapped, but the effort has to be made.

As David Eden suggests in his excellent chapter on 'The profoundly handicapped child',[3] decisions about the child's visual viewpoint 'may be decided quite simply by lying or sitting on the floor at the child's eye level'. In the same way one can get something of John's feelings of immobility and consequent frustration and dependence (page 12) by being tied up to immobilise arms and legs voluntarily. Plugs in the

38

ears and a bandage over the eyes give a starting point from which to imagine the feel of the world to a child like Angela (page 17), who moved but could not see or hear. But these exercises are only starting points for the adult's imagination.

One great advantage of teaching on Skylark Ward was the opportunity to watch a wide variety of people handling the children. It became evident that some men and women are more naturally attuned than others to observing the many bodily and facial reactions of a handicapped child, and of responding sensitively to these cues. This natural capacity to observe and to react imaginatively is not necessarily determined by any particular age, sex, social background or education. I write as a woman who has had children of her own, but this special sensitivity is *by no means* confined to motherly women. Some young men who have not fathered children may have this intuitive awareness, whereas some middle-aged mothers may not.

When I read the account of John and Elizabeth Newson's research at Nottingham on how normal babies learn to communicate and become human beings,[4] I was struck by its relevance to our work of trying to observe and communicate with profoundly handicapped people. Although the research has been concerned with normal small babies and their mothers, and although some of their conclusions might be viewed with reservations by other people, I feel their work highlights the importance of acute observation and constant interaction with the profoundly handicapped.

I summarise some of their findings here. The reader must decide on the relevance to understanding and working with people whose mental ages remain that of babies and small children, but who are deprived of the normal baby's curiosity and normal channels of sensory stimulation.

Work is being done at the Child Development Research Unit at Nottingham, and by Colwyn Trevarthen, a biological scientist at Edinburgh, and by others at Oxford, using video-tape, film, recording equipment and other technical aids, to 'capture' pictures and sounds of the small baby on his own, interacting with his mother, or with a stranger. All this underlines the individuality of each baby from birth and his intimate exchange of signals with the person who mothers him. Each baby is born with a temperament and style that is entirely his own. By careful observation his mother can not only see his individual characteristics, but she can help develop these by her way of responding to him from his first hours of life. By her sensitivity of response to his special needs and all the small clues he gives her about himself, his likes and dislikes, she enables him to grow into *this* human being, quite different from anyone else.

The Newsons claim that during the baby's first year of life, the really important thing to look for is the way he establishes a 'dialogue' through a continuing exchange of gesture signals with those who look after him during his waking hours. Mother and baby play a game of emotional ping-pong. They use the word 'dialogue' to stress that there is a continuing exchange of signals often faster than once per second. Very far from being a blank slate, the baby is born with a special built-in capacity to learn from *someone* – usually his mother, or whoever handles him consistently from birth.

The slowed-down video-recordings suggest that over the span of a second or two the baby makes a very highly organised sequence of co-ordinated actions. 'Movements of head, eyes and eyebrows, hands and fingers, together with vocalisations, are all beautifully articulated and synchronised', as if the baby were already versed in some universal language of gesticulation *long before* he can interpret the significance of other people's actions. His mother responds to these gestures, and because she gives them meaning, the baby very gradually also begins to use the gestures and sounds meaningfully, as a way of getting her attention.

Some researchers think that the normal baby makes fleeting practice smiles in response to various stimuli. Because these early smiles come and go so quickly, there has been dispute about whether they are social responses or just 'wind'. The mother, by treating them as meaningful social

40

gestures and by responding to them as real smiles, enables them to become just that. The build-up of the interaction between mother and baby is very fast once he tries out his first wobbly smiles. Smiling is the baby's insurance against being neglected. 'All human beings like to be liked. The mother whose baby smiles at her has no doubt of his affection or of his humanness.'[5]

In our society it is still the mother who normally does most of this early communicating with the baby, but a father, brother, or even a grandfather, could call forth the same responses, provided he was finely tuned to the baby's needs and individuality, handled him constantly, and was prepared to credit him with human reactions.

All the children in Skylark Ward, except those who had been totally blind from birth, responded to an adult's attention and smiles by laughing or smiling back. Even the very poorly sighted children had learnt to respond in this way. It was, however, much harder to elicit a response of this kind from some of the older patients who had for many years been in other hospitals and institutions. Given the appropriate stimulation, the Skylark children had learnt to communicate without speech in a variety of ways. It would be a mistake to credit profoundly handicapped people with feelings or a subtlety of understanding they have not learnt, but the more obvious danger is to underestimate their capacities because we have not watched them patiently, or for long enough. In this area honesty must be combined with sensitivity.

In caring for severely handicapped people who are in many ways at the same stage of development as very young, normal babies, we may need to think of developing within ourselves very sensitive antennae during our interaction with them. It is not simply a question of physical mothering but of caring as a mother does, of drawing the person forth, eliciting responses and reacting meaningfully to his tiny signals of pleasure, frustration and distress. The Newsons write: 'It may be that children's humanity has to be *made* during the interactions between them and those who already possess it.'

41

Perhaps the more we interact in this way with the profoundly handicapped and grow to love them, the more they become lovable to themselves and other people. This process makes the children more human, and makes the hard work of caring for them a satisfying experience for the adult who finds himself enriched in quite new ways. Anyone who has become deeply involved in trying to improve the lifestyle of handicapped people has evolved a way of life that is *humanising* for everyone, whether staff, parents or the initially disadvantaged person. People like Dr Kushlick in the Wessex Region, Dr Brimblecombe in Exeter and Dr Sylvester at St Lawrence's Hospital, Caterham, Surrey, and experiments in community living,[6] all point to the possibility of a spiralling interaction between the advantaged and the handicapped person so that the difference between normal and subnormal matters less (see chapter 12).

Chapter 5

HOW THE TEAM WORKED

The children and young people on Skylark were looked after by a number of people belonging to different professional groups. In this chapter I will describe how these people worked together. Although the children missed out on so many of the things a good home or hostel life can provide, it would be a mistake to overlook the many services they received from a team of qualified, dedicated people. Some of these services, things like dentistry, physiotherapy and speech therapy, are very hard to obtain if you have a handi-capped child living at home. Children from the community used, in fact, to spend time on Skylark Ward to gain the benefit of such services.

The professional people caring for the children fell into the following categories:

> Medical, psychiatry, nursing and dental staff.
> Psychologists.
> Social workers.
> Physiotherapists and speech therapists.
> Teachers, including two specialist music teachers.
> Occupational therapists.

THE PSYCHIATRIST

The ultimate responsibility for the child, while in hospital, was the psychiatrist's. The child's day-to-day medical needs were attended to by a doctor who covered several wards besides Skylark.

On Skylark we usually saw the psychiatrist at least once a week. He used to visit patients accompanied by the ward

43

doctor and he would come into the classroom during the morning to see the children. He often arrived when we were in the middle of a group activity (see page 69) and I found it very encouraging when he commented on their enjoyment, or remarked how well a child was, perhaps, stirring a cake mix. In a friendly, informal way it was easy to ask his advice about any child who was either causing us particular concern, or showing a little more alertness. Occasionally he would ask us, as school staff, to try a new approach, particularly with a child he had had brought in for a period of special observation or assessment. An illustration of this was when we had Bobby.

Bobby was a cherubic, rounded two-year-old. He was one of the sweetest-looking children I have seen anywhere. He had soft fair hair, big blue eyes and plump pink cheeks. Very sadly, he was functioning around a developmental stage equivalent to a normal six to nine months. He was very floppy with such poor muscle tone that he could not yet sit up. He lay on his back and rolled about on the mat, gurgling happily and playing with his hands and toes and any bright toys he could reach. He interacted quite spontaneously with any child he rolled up against. He could hold and shake a baby rattle. It was a delight to nurse him on one's lap and to play with him. His sight and hearing were perfect, he smiled and responded, but for a two-year-old he was obviously very retarded physically and mentally. The psychiatrist wanted us, in the classroom, to try to assess how far he would respond to continual loving attention and sensory stimulation which he might have been missing in his home. When he came into Skylark he was still having his drinks from a feeding bottle and the psychiatrist wanted him to be weaned on to a baby mug. Bobby protested strongly and tearfully at our efforts to get him to drink from a mug. After a day with us his placid, cheerful composure began to give way to long bouts of crying and he seemed to be becoming very distressed.

When the psychiatrist came to see how he was settling

down, Elizabeth and I explained our concern about his change of behaviour. We were wondering how much the transition from home to hospital was affecting Bobby. How far was he exhibiting the separation anxiety a normal two-year-old would be likely to show? We also wondered whether the removal of his feeding bottle, at this moment, was adding to the stress he felt.

It was decided to continue with the feeding mug as his mother had particularly asked for this. By the next morning Bobby had a very severe chest cold and had to be kept in bed and out of the classroom for several days. When he did come back it was hard to assess whether his apathy and general lack of *joie de vivre* were due to the infection, or whether he had been pining for home. He was in Skylark for only two weeks. When he went home he was accepting little drinks from a mug. I was left with the feeling that we might have done more for Bobby if we had had the facilities to admit him with his mother. I was able to explain my feelings about this to the psychiatrist, but it appeared that Bobby's mother would not come in with him. I relate the story in order to show that the atmosphere on Skylark was one in which inter-disciplinary exchanges were friendly with good relationships. The psychiatrist gave me much help on the occasion of Anne's death (see page 31) and in many discussions about very severely handicapped babies (see chapter 9).

THE WARD DOCTOR

The ward doctor came in to see the children at least once and often twice a day if any child was particularly unwell. It was again very helpful to be able to discuss with her the many varying effects of epileptic fits on the children. One of the constant problems of severely brain-damaged children having fits is finding the optimum level at which to maintain their anti-convulsant drugs. Too low a dosage and the fits may become so frequent and severe that they reach a dangerous state in which emergency injections are required. When, at other times, their fits lessen, it is better to reduce the drug intake and lessen the sedative side-effects. Henry was a child who would have long periods of constant grand and petit mals. He then had to be drugged into a state where it was impossible to do much with him in the classroom because he slept most of the time. Then, for no apparent reason, he would have no fits at all for several months. As a teacher, one always wanted to make the most of such a good period because then his learning capacity was at its best.

Skylark was not the right place for Lucy, a child with severe epilepsy. During her good spells she was very over-active and could walk, run, climb and use simple gymnasium apparatus. At such times we found it hard to give her all the individual attention she needed: plenty of exercise, outdoor ball games, training to come back when called and practise in giving herself her own food and drinks.

Then suddenly she would start having one grand mal after another and spend weeks in bed, drugged into a state of almost total torpor. The teaching staff were meant to watch for all fits and immediately report their length and time to the charge nurse. The doctor's advice in this area was invaluable.

THE NURSING STAFF

The nursing staff on Skylark were responsible to the charge nurse, or the deputy charge, both of whom were qualified nurses. There was always a qualified nurse on duty, but rarely more than one. The bulk of the nursing staff consisted of student and pupil nurses doing ward placements as part of their Registered Mental Nurse Subnormal or Registered Mental Nurse courses at the training school run by the hospital, and untrained nursing auxiliaries and untrained junior aids. In general, the children on Skylark and Kestrel wards required more actual nursing than those in the other hospital wards, where the patients were rarely ill. Skylark and Kestrel children were prone to bad colds, respiratory infections with a raised temperature, asthma, bronchitis, urinary infections,

46

gastro-enteritis and severe epilepsy. They had skin infections, boils, styes and nappy rashes, all of which had to be watched and treated carefully. They were delicate children and one had to take care to keep them warmly wrapped up out of doors on cold days, and very gradually exposed to the sun on warm days. Some of their drugs made them burn very easily once exposed to the sun. A child like Margaret (see page 88) needed constant nursing care, and there was often at least one other child requiring nursing in bed.

However, the main part of the nurses' duties was child care rather than clinical. Most of their time was spent washing, dressing, feeding and changing the children. Laundry had to be dispatched and put away, clothes had to be sorted and tidied. The nursing staff were responsible for buying the children's clothes, although a member of the school or the physiotherapy staff was often asked to accompany a shopping expedition to help look after the children in the shops and to fit their clothes. They were also responsible for taking children to have dental treatment (see page 52) and for emergency admission to the local district general hospital. The ward was the children's home and the charge nurse stood *in loco parentis*. He was therefore responsible for all aspects of the children's welfare and entertainment outside school or occupational therapy hours. Ward outings were arranged by the nursing staff, and they were responsible for getting children to any entertainments the hospital activities team promoted, such as bonfire night, pancake races, sports days, concerts and evening clubs. School, occupational therapy and physiotherapy staff all co-operated to help in these activities but it was the charge nurse who decided who could go, and what staff he could spare to escort the children.

It was also the charge nurse who decided who could be spared from the nursing staff to come into the classroom to help us. This tended to be an informal arrangement and resulted in our seeing most frequently the nurses who were themselves keen to come in to see what we were doing, and to play with the children under our supervision and guidance.

Some of the nurses also spent time, when they could, with the older patients, playing with them or taking them out for walks.

THE PSYCHOLOGISTS AND SOCIAL WORKERS

Our contact with psychologists and social workers was centred mainly on case conferences. For these conferences, which lasted about an hour, the full team concerned with a child met in the ward sitting-room. The senior psychologist arranged the conference and her department produced the resulting report. The child's early history was outlined by the psychiatrist or doctor and comments were invited from everyone present. Alteration in behaviour and performance was given by nursing and school staff; the social worker gave an up-to-date report on the child's home; and the physiotherapist gave her report. The psychologist's latest test on the child was also discussed. Any member of the nursing staff on the ward at the time was free to come. It was a most useful exchange and usually resulted in several specific recommendations about how to handle the child. Most people felt that it was a pity time did not allow for more frequent group conferences of this kind. But the full conference was supplemented by several other joint discussions on individual children, arranged at various intervals by the nursing, the physiotherapy and the school staff. I, personally, gained my greatest insights from the group discussions held with the physiotherapy team.

THE PHYSIOTHERAPISTS

The hospital was very fortunate in being able to employ several physiotherapists, most of whom had had a training in the Bobath method of treating severely handicapped children. On Skylark Ward the physiotherapists treated the children several times a week in the classroom. I became convinced that any teacher of a group of multiply handicapped children ought to do a course in physiotherapy as part of her basic training. With these children, physiotherapy and educational goals seemed to merge completely. I think we were particularly lucky in that our team of 'physios' was made up of extremely well-qualified and experienced young women who were generous with their time and advice and totally devoid of any kind of professional segregation. Several worked part-time as they had young children of their own. As a team they also worked in the special clinic in the local district general hospital, went out to local special schools and had often visited short-term care children in their own homes before hospitalisation. The senior physiotherapist, working with our hospital psychiatrist and senior psychologist, was responsible for helping to develop a community network of support for parents of handicapped children, which I discuss in chapter 8.

The programme I worked out for Robert (see pages 35–6) was very largely based on the help and advice of the physiotherapists. A discussion with the physiotherapist team led to the making of a large wall chart on which each child was illustrated with line drawings and written explanations of how to achieve his best remedial positions. The physiotherapist's programme for Joan (see page 63) went like this:

> Has contracture in her feet, the fibrous content stiffens, check that her boots are put on correctly.
> Try to get more total contact with her, by massaging her feet firmly.
> Try to get more eye-to-eye contact.
> Get her from prone lying on her tummy up to kneeling on all fours with head in mid-line.
> Try to get her to bear weight on her legs with and without splints leaning back against large rubber ball.
> Try to get her to look up for toys just above her eye level and reach out for them.
> Try to get her to help with her mug for drinks.
> Try to talk to her more.

It is obvious from this that the physiotherapists were able to use our classroom for their work. I would look out for toys

49

that might attract Joan; she liked for instance, large toys on wheels that she could move: trucks, cars, push-along toys. It was up to us to see that there were toys that would attract Joan, and that they were hung at a level which would make her look up and not down as was her usual, rather inward-turning reaction to things and people.

Garden netting was useful (see page 21)

The physiotherapists advised us to study Nancy Finnie's excellent book.[1] Also, every now and again, the hospital would arrange for all the staff a lecture or a film, followed by a discussion. A recent film made by the National Children's Home, in co-operation with the National Children's Bureau, on a pilot project in Gloucestershire with a group of severely handicapped (Skylark-type) children demonstrated, among many other good new ideas, a group physiotherapy session set to music.[2] Under the direction of a physiotherapist, each member of staff worked with one child in a group session, stretching arms and legs, rolling, kneeling and moving the whole body.

Within weeks of seeing the film the physiotherapists set up a similar session on Skylark, drawing in sufficient school and nursing staff to have a one-to-one session with music. It was a great success and will be repeated regularly.

It was a tremendous help that the physiotherapists worked in the classroom so that their aims, and ours, could merge naturally. In other situations where children are withdrawn from school to another building for physiotherapy it must be harder to achieve such a blending of goals. It would have helped them and us if we could have had a quiet area in which to work with individual children who were easily distracted.

THE MUSIC AND SPEECH THERAPISTS

I have referred to the work of the music teachers elsewhere (see page 71). The speech therapist worked with the one speaking Skylark child who went up to school daily. It was not possible for her to do much with my group, but her advice and expertise were available when I wanted to discuss with her any child like Hilda (page 17) or John (page 10).

THE OCCUPATIONAL THERAPISTS

The school staff had contact with the occupational therapy department when one of their team came to Skylark Ward in the afternoons to work with the older patients. Several of the older children in my group spent the mornings in school with us and the afternoons with Joseph, the occupational therapist. He had his own occupational therapy equipment and many original ways of working with a most difficult and unresponsive group of severely handicapped young adults. Amongst other things, he made them a large touch board that included about twenty different materials to produce varying tactile sensations: soft lamb's wool, coarse goat hair, suède, nail heads, rock, stretched wires, polished wood, plastic, foil and bells. He was always generous in sharing this and other equipment with us. I learnt more from Joseph about living with severely handicapped people than from almost anyone else. He had started as a nurse on Skylark before joining the occupational therapy team, and he knew all the Skylark children very well, and they knew him. John crowed with delight whenever he appeared and always wanted to be carried by him when we went on ward outings.

Joseph, in his twenties, with university experience, unmarried, had that quality of empathy with handicapped people that I tried to describe in chapter 4. He was an unconventional young man, impatient of bureaucratic attitudes, an original thinker, and one of the generation of young people who, like Geoffrey and the other college volunteers (see pages 26–7) will eventually be responsible for changing society's attitudes to mental handicap. I liked his robust, masculine, matter-of-fact approach and his avoidance of over-protectiveness. These blended with his sensitivity and love for the children, in ways a woman may find hard to achieve.

THE DENTIST

The final person to mention, in the caring team, was the dentist. The children all had regular inspections by the dentist and his assistant and this sometimes happened in the classroom. At first I was a bit surprised and wondered whether it would be better for the children to be seen outside the classroom. Later, I realised, it afforded a teaching opportunity which could be used to reinforce the children's awareness of their teeth, mouths, tongues and lips. I will refer to this again, in the next chapter on the children's self-awareness.

Any actual dentistry, like fillings or extractions, had to be done under a general anaesthetic. For this the child was wheeled over to the dental department by a member of the ward staff. When it was John's turn to go across, I used to try

52

to explain to him why he had missed his breakfast. As the whole experience frightened and upset him, it was difficult to know how far he would benefit by being prepared for the experience. When he returned we used to keep him wrapped up in blankets in a big hospital pram in a corner of the classroom, and talk to him soothingly as he recovered from the effects of the anaesthetic and the total experience.

Before ending this chapter I should like to emphasise again the importance of working as a team. Of course there were occasions when communication between various members of the caring staff was less than perfect. Perhaps I have presented a picture of how it should be and how it was at its best. What I learnt was the importance of making friends with every newcomer to the ward, whatever his position in the 'hierarchy'. I learnt much, for instance, from the overseas nurses. The hospital employed many people from Mauritius, Sri Lanka, Malaysia and other eastern countries. There were dedicated nurses from many parts of Africa and from Scandinavia. All these people were outstanding for their gentle empathy with handicapped people.[3]

Chapter 6

THE CHILD'S AWARENESS OF 'SELF'

It seems pointless to discuss the child's awareness of self, without first underlining the need for one's own self-awareness as the caring adult. One of the many things I learnt from living on Skylark Ward was the necessity to come to terms with my own emotions, body and sexuality, if I was to work with these children effectively. If you are afraid of your own body and bodily feelings, you will be afraid of theirs. I only gradually became aware of what was happening to me. Some of the other staff, like Joseph (see page 52) were much more naturally at ease with themselves than I was when I started on Skylark.

The whole business of looking after heavily dependent people is very *physical*. Depending on one's background, it can be difficult at first to immerse oneself in a daily round that must involve an enormous amount of physical contact. As well as actually coping with vomit, dribbling, copious catarrh, filthy nappies and bodies, revolting smells, one must be able to *use* one's body in every way to reach these children. Inhibitions about rolling about the floor with a large patient, cradling large physically unattractive boys and girls, feeling, stroking, caressing, and being felt, stroked and caressed, all have to go. It was difficult to react gently when a child's involuntary flexor spasm, or startle reflex, soaked you with a sticky drink. I still hate being suddenly thumped on the back by a more robust patient – my initial response to this is still an angry one. I hate being caught unawares!

54

It was the physiotherapists who taught me that cerebral palsied children have a poor knowledge of their bodies because often they have not been able to explore them with their hands, chew their toes, clap their hands or pull their hair as a normal baby does. With spastic children, any effort often makes the spasticity worse thus restricting their movements still further because of discomfort and fear of pain. In the end, unless treatment is given, they do not want to move at all because their abnormal movements make them feel afraid and insecure. Often these children either do not pass through the normal stages of a baby's development, or get stuck at one early stage and so are deprived of early normal sensory experience. Sometimes they are further deprived of this experience by the adults who handle them, over-protecting them and treating them as fragile babies. Mothers may be afraid of the unnatural movements and responses the children make. All movements are learnt through sensation so if sensory experience is denied, movements will be impaired. Watch, for instance, a normal small child trying to crawl under a chair. It learns that it is too small a space to get through, not by looking at the chair, but by trying and banging his head. In this way the normal child learns concepts about himself in space which the spastic child is unable to learn.

It followed from this that much of our work in the school room centred around giving the children the normal sensory experiences they had missed, so that they became more conscious of the different parts of their bodies, were trained to make purposeful movements and became more aware of themselves as individual people.[1]

Before starting to work with a child I would try to make him aware of *me* as a person. I held his hand, spoke his name, and tried to establish eye contact. This might take several minutes. I might then pick him up, explaining what we were going to do in simple clear language. I might carry him to the long mirror and sitting in front of it, feel and name all the main parts of his body, and holding his hand get him to feel and stroke my face and hands and body. From this we might go and sit on the mat to work through a simple piece of apparatus together. All the time he would be feeling my body against his, hearing my voice speaking to him. During individual work with a child it was essential, although at times very difficult, to concentrate on him to the exclusion of everyone else in the room. We used screens to shut out the other sights and sounds as far as possible. As well as being humorous and loving it was necessary to be consistent and firm in handling each child. Because many of their movements were involuntary, and because their understanding of language was so limited, one had to combine immense patience with a determination not to tolerate behaviour which, with your help and understanding, they could control. It was surprising how many of the children understood a 'No!' when combined with a look that implied strong dissatisfaction.

Confusion over body image and the question of how to discipline fairly are well illustrated by John's behaviour at certain times. Notes on his earlier behaviour said that he was prone to temper tantrums. After months of careful observation we correlated his physical condition with his periods of lassitude and tantrums. If there was enough ward time to sit John on a chair commode at regular intervals he would probably rarely wet or soil a nappy. He had enough understanding to recognise unacceptable behaviour and he probably had some degree of physical control. We discovered that his periods of unco-operative languor and pale complexion were correlated with periods of acute constipation, due, no doubt, to his holding back of regular bowel motions. After five blank days he was treated and then went through periods of acute distress as the laxative, or enema, stirred things up inside. We tried to soothe him by rubbing his tummy, and one realised what a terrifying feeling the pain

56

must have been to a child who is unable to understand what is going on inside his own body.

Sometimes he became disturbingly frantic. He would kick wildly in all directions, flail with his arms and foam at the mouth with shuddering jaws. Alternatively he would roll himself into a tight ball, and clench his arms to his head. He would look fearfully 'angry' with beetling brows. He was, of course, in a state of pain and panic, and it looked like a temper tantrum. If these periods of uncontrolled behaviour had been viewed as tantrums in the past, and frowned upon by adults, John's dilemma must have been made more acute. Here was something awful happening to his body: it was giving him quite different messages from usual, yet instead of sympathy and understanding he was met with harsh looks, words of admonition and possibly rejection by adults.

The difficulty in handling John was that he could behave very temperamentally. He liked a lot of attention and could look very angry while I worked with other children. He had learnt some voluntary control of his limbs and moods and with direction could inhibit some of his wilder athetoid movements. The physiotherapists wanted us to encourage him to sit quietly at times, with his head in midline and his feet resting firmly on the floor or against a wedge. Left to himself he would try to attract attention. He moved his knees up and down and, when sitting in a wheelchair, rubbed his right heel in particular against the back of his foot-rest pulling his shoe off. This meant his right shoe fastening was constantly in need of repair through the shoe being forced off his foot.

One morning, at breakfast, one of the senior nurses had reprimanded him for getting his shoes off. John arrived in school that morning sobbing uncontrollably. The nurse had gone to late breakfast. We could do nothing with him until the nurse reappeared and told us what had happened. The incident illustrated John's sensitivity to an adult's displeasure, and the difficulty of disciplining these children fairly.

John, Hilda, Lucy (see page 46), and several other children had learnt the meaning of some simple directions, like, 'look at me', 'hold your head up', 'stretch your arm out'. But one had to allow them time in which to respond. We did a lot of things to reinforce the meanings of 'up' and 'down'. We played singing games, with actions, such as 'the grand old Duke of York' and other nursery rhymes. The Play School television programmes demonstrated a lot of simple bodily movements to music and we used to move the children's limbs as they watched.

In all these activities we were trying, under physiotherapy guidance, to help establish the memory of correct movement patterns, and to undo incorrect movement patterns which the child had established in his past.

Sense of personal identity

All personal interactions with a child could be used to re-emphasise his importance as an individual. We used their names constantly and always tried to talk to them whatever we were doing with them, or to them. Lifting in and out of wheelchairs could be done with a verbal commentary, with dignity and courtesy. We were lucky in having a young woman hairdresser, who came regularly, with her own normal little boy, to cut the children's hair. This took a whole morning, but we put a floral wrap on each child in turn and let them have plenty of time to look in a hand mirror and in the long wall mirror.

Maternal and sexual awareness

Several of the older girls loved small babies. We used to help them hold, and use rattles to play with, some of the less handicapped, more responsive little children in for short-term care.

Several of the older boys and girls showed clear evidence of sexual feeling for staff of the opposite sex. I was astonished

58

when a hitherto very unresponsive lad of twenty, sitting on the seat beside me at a concert, suddenly turned, embraced me and heaved himself on to my lap.

I felt all these natural feelings could have been met much more effectively in a 'family' grouping, such as I outline in chapter 11. Here was potential for awareness of 'self' which we were not beginning to explore or extend.

Teasing

The children loved simple jokes and laughter. Sometimes inexperienced nursing staff did not realise how confused John got when verbal teasing took the form of pretending he was not going to do something we had told him he was going to do. I remember the distress he showed when a nurse said, jokingly, 'of course everyone is going to the pantomime, except John!' It was a question of knowing the children. Hilda could, in fact, take a lot more verbal ribbing than John. Their sense of humour was individual – as yours and mine is.

Self-help

To increase their self-awareness, their self-confidence and feeling of personal worth it seemed essential to try to increase the children's ability to help themselves, if only a very little more than before. All the children had difficulty in carrying out to demand the different voluntary movements of their lips and tongues, or in imitating such movements in others. Through touch we wanted to make the children more aware of muscle tone and feel the movement of their lips, jaws and tongues. This seemed an obvious area in which one might teach them a little more self-help. This was how we came to work out a self-help drinks programme.

What kind of self-help could one teach these children? I decided that it might be possible to teach them to hold their own mugs and give themselves their own drinks. Some handicapped children find it easier to drink by sucking through straws. In an American hospital I saw a child who had no use of his arms drink very successfully and unaided through a right-angled straw once the mug had been placed on the floor beside him. Unfortunately none of the Skylark children had the capacity to suck in this way, nor, indeed, to blow bubbles through a straw.

I am giving a detailed account of our drinks programme because it illustrates the very small stages through which one must go to teach severely handicapped children the elements of a single new skill. I never expected the whole group to become independent in drinking but I felt all the children would gain something, at their own level, by taking part in such a project. The programme highlighted the individual strengths and weaknesses of each child. It stressed the length of time, the patience and continual persistence that such a programme demands if it is to be properly carried through. It could be used as a method for setting-up a self-feeding programme; or, with slightly less-handicapped children, it could be a programme for self-dressing, washing, hair brushing and more ambitious steps towards personal independence. It underlines the importance of having enough time to let these children go at *their* pace, and not at a rate directed by adult schedules.

Observation

The first stage in the programme was a period of individual observation of each child, to see how far he could already help himself. Previously, it had always been assumed that they were totally dependent and drinks were given in baby mugs with spouts attached. Drinks were often given at a very fast rate so that the children could be got through as quickly as possible. They were also sometimes given at a most inappropriate angle because the child happened, at that moment, to be lying on his back or on his stomach. In our classroom there was plenty of time to let each child drink at his own rate, and with physiotherapist guidance, in his most comfortable, remedial position.

Assessment

Detailed observation showed that the children fell into four main groups:

1 Those who were almost independent.
2 Those who still needed much encouragement to help themselves.
3 Children who needed skilled physiotherapist guidance in order to drink more easily.
4 Those who could not help themselves except in a token way.

Instructions

We made out a very large wall chart with the children divided into these four groups and with detailed directions about each child. I went through the chart with everyone, including volunteers, who came into the classroom to help give the mid-morning and mid-afternoon drinks. For the weekends and school holidays I made a similar smaller chart and tied it to the drinks trolley in the hope that it would be used by the hospital staff in our absence.

The children

Readers may be interested to see how the children described in the individual profiles earlier in the book, fell into the different categories. Some children not in the profiles are also mentioned here, again with changes of names and characteristics in order to preserve their anonymity.

61

Group 1. Those who were almost independent.

Dick had very poor sight but had already been trained at home. He seemed to see a large orange, two-handled mug, better than any other object. As one approached saying 'Dick, here is your drink', he held out his left hand. He held his mug in his left hand, slightly supported with the right. We stood by him while he drank to prevent him dropping the mug when he finished drinking or had had enough. We encouraged him to hand the mug back when finished, being lavish with praise if he did. He liked long drinks, preferring blackcurrant to any other flavour.

Lucy was very variable in her aptitudes as she suffered from severe epilepsy. When she was having a good phase with no fits she was quite capable of drinking unaided. During an epileptic phase she became reduced to a state of total dependency. It was important, therefore, to remember to let her drink unaided once she was in a better phase again.

Pamela (see page 20). We sat her well up in a good sitting position, saying firmly to get her attention 'Here's your drink, Pamela, hold it properly'. We used a small two-handled mug with lid and spout, only half-full. We clasped the fingers of both her hands firmly round the handles, as she otherwise had a sloppy hold, and was inclined to let drink dribble away down her feeder. She drank very little, very slowly. She could be left for a brief period, but needed her concentration reinforced frequently. We tried to get her to hand the mug back.

Jane was less severely spastic than many in the group, although she had very weak legs and never learnt to stand or walk unaided. She had a considerable amount of manual dexterity and enjoyed putting small toys into larger containers. We would get her into a good sitting position and remove all toys from her vicinity. We spoke to her clearly: 'Jane, here is your drink', and then put a single-handled mug into whichever hand she held out, as she was ambidextrous. We got her to support the mug with the other hand as her grip was inclined to be sloppy, and stood by her to prevent her dropping it. We prevented her trying to touch us while she was drinking, but remained near her in order to prevent her turning the full mug upside down, or dropping it while still full. Her concentration needed to be focused on the mug. Jane liked to be dependent and made constant efforts to secure attention, including an angry response when she deliberately dropped the mug. If she did drop the full mug we tried to show no response, mopped her and the mess up, and removed her into a corner of the room with no toys and turned our attention to another child.

Lucinda had very poor sight. She disliked physical contact with people or things, but was quite capable of holding a single-handled mug in her right hand and drinking from it. She needed slight support underneath the mug to prevent her dropping it, or throwing it right away. We gave her much verbal encouragement, and tried to get her to hand the mug back.

Group 2. Those who still needed much encouragement to help themselves.

Henry (see page 27). We sat him up well, and focused his attention on the mug – a two-handled one without a top. We clasped his fingers round the handles. He had a much firmer grip with the left hand. He needed help but we left him alone as much as possible. We allowed him to drink slowly so that he did not choke. He sat well on one's lap and it was sometimes easier to teach him in this position.

Joan (see page 49) was a very low-grade mongol child. She was very floppy and totally unaccustomed to helping herself. However as she enjoyed grasping toys she could have her fingers fastened round the handles of a mug, and it was worth persisting with this in the hope that she would show more initiative in time.

Group 3. Children who needed skilled physiotherapist guidance in order to drink more easily. In the classroom Elizabeth and I spent our time helping the children in this group, and left the other staff to do the rest of the children.

Hilda (see page 16) was an extremely difficult child to give food or drink to. She hated the inexpensive brands of orange squash which were the usual drinks. She preferred black-currant juice and loved milk drinks. She tended to spit out a drink she disliked, sometimes at a new person on the ward whom she thought she might 'take for a ride'. With phy-siotherapist help we learnt that the best way to control Hilda was to get her side-sitting on the floor with the adult behind her to inhibit the constant backward thrust of her body. Having bent Hilda forward from the waist, her arms would relax and it sometimes became possible to get her to clasp the fingers of one hand round the handles of the mug and help to raise it to her mouth. An alternative way of managing her was to sit in a broad armchair with Hilda also in the chair but between one's legs. In any position one had to be on guard against her immense startle reflex. Anyone coming into the room or someone speaking suddenly would make Hilda jump, invariably soaking the helper and herself with her drink. To be angry was an inappropriate response as she had no voluntary control over this reflex. It was, therefore, much better to try to remove her to a quiet corner of the room before giving her a drink.

John (see page 10) very much wanted to help himself with his hands, but the effort stiffened his hand and throat muscles so much that it was a self-defeating exercise. With the help of the physiotherapists and the excellent chart, produced by the Hornsey College of Art,[2] we learnt how to stroke his throat to relax his muscles before offering a drink. The next step was to stand behind John to inhibit the very strong, involuntary, backward thrust of his head when offered a drink. In order to have both hands free to give him the drink I had to use my body to support his head in an upright position. I would then spread the fingers of my right hand (as shown by the physiotherapist) two under John's chin, and then the other two above and below his mouth in

64

order to keep his jaws closed. I used to say, 'Keep your mouth shut, John, but just open your lips like a letter box.' I then put the mug edge against his lower lip, tilted the juice towards his lips and encouraged him to suck it up in little sips and swallow slowly. Unless one let in very small sips at a time his tendency was to take in too large a mouthful, choke, splutter and gulp wind which later gave him acute indigestion and discomfort. It took five minutes to give John a drink.

Robert (see page 24). His eating and drinking was affected by his spasticity in very much the same way as John's. So we used the same technique with Robert. Unlike John, he did not have enough understanding to co-operate with verbal instructions. However the thrust in his jaws and neck muscles was less pronounced, and provided his head was well supported in an upright position he got his food and drinks down a little more easily than John did.

Group 4. Finally, there was a large number of children, including Angela (see page 17), for whom one could do little more than get them into comfortable upright positions and give them drinks, slowly, gently, lovingly as one would rather small babies, trying to make it a pleasurable experience and one that gave an opportunity for individual caring.

THE VALUE OF THE SELF-HELP DRINKS PROGRAMME

The results of the programme are difficult for me to assess. It was not done as a scientific project, set up or assessed by the psychology department. However, as a direct consequence of having the programme, the psychology department drew up a limited self-feeding programme (see page 102) and it was generally established that *given enough time and staff co-operation* many children loosely described as 'totally dependent' may, on careful analysis, prove to have limited capabilities to do more for themselves. This again, given the right conditions, can be built upon. Certainly, the more

65

independent children in group 1 gradually improved as a result of not being given unnecessary adult help.

Many of the hospital staff realised that there was some value in allowing the children to take their time, and there was more individual interaction with the children during the drinks periods. Many also began to see that although children might never become totally independent, it was better for them to be encouraged to help themselves as much as they could. Staff began to take the children on their laps, or generally make them more comfortable, rather than just pouring the drink down their throats in whatever position they happened to be when the drinks trolley arrived.

With the continual encouragement of the physiotherapists, who also helped with some of the meals as part of their regular work, the children in group 3 were being given food and drink in better remedial positions and in more comfortable ways.

When a new teacher took over the group on my departure she found the programme had a good basis; she reassessed the children and up-dated the programme accordingly.

The chief difficulty in carrying through a programme of this kind in a large ward is the need for continual vigilance and direction by one or two people. I know that when the classroom closed, at weekends and during school holidays, the new nursing staff and casual help might remain totally unaware that a drinks programme was in existence. Even in the classroom, one had to remind staff tactfully that certain children were practically independent, otherwise there was a wholesale assumption that all patients had to be 'done' as if they were still totally dependent. On the other hand, staff members who remained on the ward long enough saw the value of checking the wall chart if they could not immediately remember whether, for instance, Henry was better with his left or his right hand. They also realised the value of much verbal encouragement and praise for any effort a child made.

Given a free choice, I would have used milk-based drinks, especially in the winter months, rather than the cheap brands

66

of orange, lemon, lime and blackcurrant squash which seemed to sting the children's throats. They all seemed to enjoy warm Horlicks, Ovaltine, chocolate or milky coffee and swallowed these with much less choking and spluttering. In really hot weather we sometimes gave children water as the best thirst quencher.

When talking about 'improving the quality of life' of such children, a nice warm drink, on a cold winter's morning, with cold hands helping to clasp the warm mug seems to be a worthwhile small goal to be aimed at – a real concept and not a 'fuzzy' one.

Chapter 7

GROUP ACTIVITIES

After a period of observation and individual assessment, I made a programme of work for each child in the group, as described in an earlier chapter. This programme covered their particular achievements, general aims, suggestions for apparatus and special points to remember. It was essential that each child should have this individual programme followed through, daily if possible, according to the amount of time and help available.

However, I felt it necessary to devise some group activities in addition to the individual programmes for two reasons. The first was a question of manpower. For the first eighteen months with the group I had no classroom assistant. I had seventeen multiply handicapped children to educate with the assistance of a junior aid, an untrained girl of seventeen to eighteen years, plus such help as the nursing staff could spare from their duties. The available help was inevitably variable in number and spasmodic in time, and therefore not easy to use really effectively in sustaining each child's individual programme. Yet it was very useful for short group activities. Second, I felt the children needed the experience of being part of a stimulated group in addition to the individual stimulation. There proved to be many ways in which one could carry through aspects of the child's individual programme through the organising of a group activity.

MAYPOLE DANCING

One May Day it was cold and wet. As we could not go out of doors as planned, we made a maypole out of a coat and hat

68

stand from which we normally suspended a variety of toys for the children to play with. We cleared these off and tied four broad, bright tapes, each about four yards long – black, white, red and blue. We sewed small bells to the tapes and made a loop at the end through which a child's hand could be slipped. I found a long lacy dress in the dressing-up box. Washed, starched and ironed it looked lovely on Hilda who was the May Queen. We made a garland of blossom for her hair. John, of course, had to be the May King in a splendid cherry-red velvet cloak and a gold paper crown. We dressed them both in front of the long mirror to their very evident satisfaction! A music teacher and a volunteer came, as promised, to play their guitars. We cleared half of our very large classroom and then grouped the children so that they could all see the maypole.

The joy of this kind of amusement was that almost everyone on the ward found time to come and join in. We wanted every child to have a turn at holding a ribbon and dancing the full sequence of winding the tapes right up and back again, so we needed a lot of help. Someone had to sit at the base of the coat stand to hold it steady. The children all took part in their most appropriate ways. The three semi-ambulant children each had two members of staff to help them walk, the little ones were carried and the rest were pushed in their chairs. We danced the full sequence five times and the King and Queen each got an extra turn, leading off the first dance and bringing it to a glorious close.

I do not think we have ever been so puffed, but the more we danced and chased and wound up and back, the more the children became aware of the excitement. At the end when all the adults collapsed in exhaustion the general level of stimulation among the children was marvellous. The mid-morning drinks were brought in and we were giving these when the medical head of the unit arrived to do his weekly ward round. Totally unaware of what had happened, he came into the room with the charge nurse. He looked round at the flushed, happy faces of the children and said. 'Whatever has been

69

going on? They all look so alive this morning.' 'We've been dancing the maypole,' said Mrs D. the ward housekeeper who simply loved an opportunity to dance, which she did with great éclat in her pale green nylon overall, 'we've had a smashing morning.'

That May remained cold and grey, but we danced the indoors maypole four times during it. From this evolved some simple square-dancing in wheelchairs as another group activity.

BIRTHDAY COOKING

I found it a useful principle to base a group activity on something John understood and enjoyed. As he was by far the most intelligent child in the group, this meant that all the others joined in and got from it what they could. I hoped, in this way, to extend their capabilities and range of awareness. It meant that although only John fully understood what we were doing, all the rest got something from the activity.

Birthdays were an obvious opportunity to strengthen a child's self-awareness. They all grew to love cooking, so we usually spent a birthday making and icing the birthday cake. We grouped a number of small tables together and covered the centre one with a clean sheet. As many children as possible sat in low ordinary chairs pulled up to the tables, wedged where necessary with cushions, their feet resting on the ground or on wedges. On the centre table we laid out all the cooking equipment – a packet of instant cake mix, an egg, a large plastic mixing bowl, a wooden spoon, milk in a small jug, two round baking tins, a square of fat to grease them with and an egg whisk.

I put the egg in a hen's nest which I made with hay in a box, and showed it to all the children so they could feel the cool brown eggs with their hands, or against their cheeks. I used to tell them about hens laying eggs. I stood by the centre table and called them all by name to watch while someone helped to rip the packets open and tip the mix into the bowl.

70

Very slowly I cracked the egg against the side of the bowl and held it up high for them to watch the yolk and white drop into the bowl. Sometimes the birthday child helped to break the egg in this way. We let them see and feel the empty shell. After that the mixing began.

We passed the bowl round the circle and helped each child to beat the mixture with a wooden spoon or egg whisk. We made great jokes about 'no dribbling in the mixture – *please*!' It took a long time as we tried to give them three turns each of beating, but gradually hands reached out to grab at the bowl for their turn, and they all became aware of something interesting happening – the odd taste of uncooked mixture helped! Sometimes we borrowed the ward electric food-mixer and brought it in on a trolley to give the mixture a final boost. Some of the children especially enjoyed hearing the high-pitched whirring and the variation of speeds from slow to maximum.

A little group, including the birthday child, finally took the tins into the ward kitchen where Mrs D. would have the oven ready for the cake.

While we waited for it to cook, we brought in a bowl of washing-up water and got them to help wash and dry up all the utensils. Then a second posse went to smell the cake and bring it back from the kitchen.

After lunch we iced and decorated the cake in the same way and, finally, we lit the candles, and sang and ate the cake. Often we were able to arrange a little music at this point in order to sing more than 'Happy birthday to you' (which goes very well to the tune of 'Cum-Baya' by way of a change).

MUSIC SESSIONS

We were extremely lucky to have regular music sessions: about four half-hours a week with trained music teachers who had some experience of the Nordoff–Robbins Music Therapy methods;[1] also informal sessions when the hospital chaplain, volunteers or nursing staff would play a guitar for the children.

For group music, we brought in as many nursing staff as possible, so that, ideally, each child was helped to play an instrument: chime bars, triangles, glockenspiel, maracas, drums, bells, cymbals, castanets, while the teacher played the tune on the guitar, piano, recorder or piano accordion. The teacher introduced a wide variety of music to the children, rhythmic West Indian songs, French folk tunes and traditional nursery rhymes. There was some small group work with chime bars or drums. One teacher had a lovely singing voice and sang to the children. There was individual work with children who showed a response to a particular type of music. One very sad, withdrawn child smiled her rare smiles when played some plaintive or soft music. From our experience the provision of instrumental music in this setting is one of the best ways of reaching handicapped children of all kinds, and bringing them the happiness of communication.

My assistant, Elizabeth, and I have one very cherished memory of a glorious spring day when we were all out in the garden. Suddenly three music students walked across the lawn towards us. The children sat in rapt silence as they played 'Greensleeves' and other traditional folk airs, with flute, oboe and French horn.

GAMES

Simple group games all had something to teach the children. They were good ways of celebrating birthdays, and were particularly appropriate when we had school children, volunteers of about sixteen, who found it difficult to know how to play with profoundly handicapped, non-speaking children.

'Musical parcel'

Sometimes we wrapped a present in many layers of coloured paper, each tied loosely with a bow of string or ribbon. As the

72

parcel went round the circle, the children became gradually aware of 'my turn coming' – Pamela and Jane (see page 62) became as skilled as normal five-year-olds in removing the paper and string unaided. We usually rigged the unwrapping so that either the birthday child, or someone else who needed a morale booster was the winner. I think this game helped several of the children get much more enjoyment out of unwrapping their birthday and Christmas parcels, and it developed a sense of curiosity and exploration, as well as being good practice in manipulative skills. When we all went to the big school for the annual Christmas party our children participated much more actively in this game after three years of practice!

'Blowing egg shells'

This was a game we watched on a BBC Play School pro-gramme. Afterwards we gathered the children around the water trough. Each child had his name written in felt-tip pen on a clean half-egg shell which floated on the water like a tiny boat. Each child had an adult partner – Mrs D. and other nursing staff loved this game! The adult had to blow the child's egg shell forward through a plastic straw. We played the game in several heats until there was a final winner. It was impossible to teach these children to blow effectively, but some used to try. They loved to watch our efforts, and they learnt something about the effects of blowing.

'Grandmother's footsteps'

This is a game in which the helpers either wheeled a chair or carried a child quietly towards the 'grandmother's' back; anyone seen moving when she turned round had to go back and start again. The semi-ambulant children were helped to walk, if we had enough helpers.

'Catch the spinning platter'

This game can also be played with a circle of children in wheelchairs. Someone spins a tin plate and calls out two children's names. With an adult pushing they go forward and the helper tries to catch the plate first, before it stops spinning.

GARDENING

We did this as an indoor or outdoor activity. We had a small, sheltered, sunny yard that opened off the classroom through large glass doors. In the spring, before it was warm enough to take them outside, we would group all the children in the yard, or in the sunlight by the open doors. We spread newspapers all over the floor and put a variety of bowls and other containers filled with dry earth on tables in front of the children.

They helped us to prepare the soil by watering it with bright plastic cans, scratching it with little rakes and trowels. Great excitement when the odd worm or earwig appeared! They loved to squelch damp earth with their hands. We helped them sow the seeds: nasturtiums, pansies, radishes, lettuces, parsley, mustard and cress, runner beans, sweet peas and garden peas. When the beans and peas were an inch high the children helped us to transplant them to grow up lattice work and poles in the yard. By late spring the yard was full of greenery and flowers. John and several others loved to water the seeds and watch the small plants grow.

As the weather grew warmer we used the garden that had been made for us outside the classroom. Here the children could sit propped up, or lie over wedges by the flower beds to sow seeds and string cotton to protect them from the birds. Young volunteers enjoyed helping the children weed the rockery. The children loved to lie and roll on the grass, or let the shadows of the bushes move across their faces. John liked

74

to pick daisies and make daisy chains. Sometimes we organised simple treasure hunts with Easter eggs or other sweets in bright paper, to encourage the children to feel among clumps of daffodils or later the lovely smelling wallflowers, or reach up to pick them out of the small bushes. Out here, on really hot days we had an immense paddling pool in which they could lie and kick, or sit spooning up the water. Afterwards they would lie on the grass to sunbathe.

WALL PROJECTS

John loved to anticipate and to follow up annual events such as Christmas, Easter, outings to the zoo or sea and bonfire night, by helping us to make large wall charts. Having chosen a theme we cut out pictures or shapes and grouped the children so that they could help us to do some cutting and pasting. We made each child watch while we stuck 'his shape' on the wall. This meant that he had to extend the range of his vision, and we tried to get him to indicate where he would like his picture fixed. We did a very colourful picture of circles and rounds cut from scraps of wallpaper left over when the ward was redecorated, and suggested by a Play School programme. We did a rather ambitious one about the sea cut from a series of Sunday newspaper colour supplements, that illustrated raging seas as well as calm ones, shipwrecks, lighthouses, lightships and a collage of sea shells, nets and driftwood collected on a seaside outing.

If John learnt new things, if children used their hands to cut and paste, if volunteers found the activity meaningful and if the walls looked brighter, such projects seemed justified. It would have been pointless to have done them unless the children had participated to some degree and at their own levels of understanding.

TELEVISION

The ward acquired a very good, colour television set in the day-room. It became part of our school programme to move

75

some children through, two or three times a week to watch Play School, and a more recent series, devised for pre-school children, called 'You and me'. We had several aims in doing this. First, we selected children who could see the screen and for whom we wanted to encourage a better sitting position, usually in ordinary low chairs with small tables in front of them. For them the programme provided a focal point of interest and made them sit with less support. Second, many of the simple body movements set to music on the programmes could, with adult help, be imitated by the children. Third, we picked up many ideas of simple craft activities which we later carried out with the children in the classroom.

One week, Play School showed children how to paint rainbow pictures. This consisted of brushing over a sheet of white paper with ordinary water and then painting a rainbow in sweeping arcs of the correct colours on the damp paper.

Later in the classroom I told the children the story of Noah's Ark using a large wooden ark with animals and people. Several of the children were then helped to paint rainbow pictures and listen to the record with the simple rainbow refrain.[2] As Play School always asks its child viewers to send in their paintings, we sent off the rainbow pictures that had been done by John, Hilda, Pamela and Henry. I sent a covering letter explaining who the children were and how much they enjoyed the programme. A week or so later, imagine our excitement when the Play School lady pointed out a great screen of rainbow pictures in the studio, including our four pictures. John nearly died of excitement! A few days later the BBC sent special Play School greetings cards, with a handwritten message to each of our seventeen children. We stuck them all in their own birthday books.

In the same way, having explained the Queen's silver wedding anniversary to the children, we watched the programme and sent her a card made by the children, with a covering letter of explanation about the group. Once again we got back a personal reply from Buckingham Palace to thank the children of Skylark Ward!

One blustery March day a nursing auxiliary said: 'I've found an old kite. Let's take the children outdoors and see if they enjoy watching it fly!'

A tall volunteer soon had the kite up in the air, tugging against its string. We had got most of the children out in their wheelchairs well wrapped up. We laid their hands along the kite string in turn so that they became aware of its tugging action.

Gradually bowed heads lifted, stiff necks stretched, eyes followed our pointing fingers and the children began to smile and laugh as the red, green and white kite floated high above their ward.

Suddenly the kite flopped to the ground, and there followed more exclamations of delight and dismay. An enterprising nurse lengthened the tail with a piece of bandage and away it went again. We tied the kite to the chairs in turn so that the children could feel themselves being pulled along – John crowed with delight at this new sensation. As with the maypole dancing, the children were excited and stimulated by a new experience that had arisen by pure chance.

On another occasion when we were joined by a group of more able children from another class (see page 79) we had a very successful afternoon. On this occasion we had been given two new kites that were held by a steering bar attached to two strings. Again the wind was strong and the children needed an adult's help to hold the kites, but the effort of wrestling with the wind encouraged hesitant speech and physical movement. This time the children watched the unique swooping flight of great scarlet and lemon 'bats' clear-cut against a backcloth of bright blue sky and massed banks of curling white clouds above green tree-tops.

Here were possibilities to be explored. If man's primaeval dream is to fly, to shake off the earth, to commit himself to the atmosphere in silent, soaring flight, kite flying could be a very special activity for handicapped people. That afternoon children of very varying abilities had joined in a group game from which each had gained something at his own level. The more able had enjoyed helping children like John, Hilda and Pamela.

Chapter 8

THE WIDER WORLD

Unless one has worked on a ward like Skylark it is almost impossible to visualise how much these children need the outside world brought to them. The staff, too, welcomed any visitors from outside. This feeling of being isolated from the mainstream of life was emphasised by the physical environment of Skylark. The summer was different. We could take the children outside and see other people moving about the hospital grounds. But on dark, grey winter days when the wind howled round the ward and the rain fell in sheets across the great plain of grass obscuring even the other buildings, one felt incredibly cut off. On such an afternoon the arrival of student volunteers, soaked to the skin after a bicycle ride of several miles against a head wind, to play with the children seemed like a small miracle of generosity.

How the outside world came to Skylark can perhaps be seen as a series of concentric circles of people.

MIXING WITH LESS-HANDICAPPED CHILDREN

On leaving Skylark Ward I was put in charge of a class of much brighter, physically able children in the main school building. It was possible to arrange a few sessions like the kite-flying episode described in the last chapter. Under careful supervision, and with constant training, the abler children could be taught to wheel the chairs of the physically handicapped ones, and they enjoyed the responsibility of doing this. With this abler group we had regular music sessions with the Kestrel children. It was interesting to see how the abler children gradually overcame their initial

79

reluctance to help a physically contorted child beat a drum, a chime bar or shake a tambourine. Like us, these children disliked the messiness and smell of dribble, saliva and sickness. But with encouragement they eventually found real satisfaction in helping and the sessions were very successful for all the children and staff.

Because any institutional life is something of a jungle in which the individual learns to fight for survival, it was necessary to teach the able children to be generous – to share their sweets and toys – and be kind to their weaker brethren! I saw a little of this kind of education and the self-fulfilment and self-confidence it could give to both the abler and the more handicapped child.

When the adult patients in the occupational therapy department gave a Christmas show for the rest of the hospital, it was delightful to watch the enjoyment of children like John seeing people he knew 'playing the fool', singing and performing. This particular annual event seemed to mean more to our children than any of the other entertainments put on by various generous groups of young people from the local community.

THE CHILDREN'S FAMILIES

When the children made their cards at Christmas and Easter to send home to their families, we played a game with them, putting their letters inside a toy mail van and running it along to the doll's house. Here the postman knocked at the door, which was answered by a peg-doll lady – 'John's Mummy', 'Hilda's Mummy' and so on round the children. We made the doll say: 'Oh! how lovely! a card from John' or 'from Hilda', naming all the children in turn. Sometimes Elizabeth and I did the same mime using the wendy house. She would act the postmaid and I would be the mother inside.

When letters, cards and parcels came from home for the children we acted out the reverse procedure of Mummy posting to them and the letters coming by mail van to the hospital.

Establishing links for the children with the world outside depended partly on the strength of their families' relationships with them. On Skylark we saw the whole spectrum, ranging from Dick's parents who only agreed to his coming into hospital at all because one of them was, at the time, seriously ill, and on the specific condition that he would go home every weekend and part of each school holiday; to Bernard whose family had lost all contact with him. In between these two extremes were children who received letters and presents from home with one or two visits a year, and other children who were in much closer contact, being visited every three or four weeks, perhaps being taken out for the day; and some who went home for a few days each school holiday. The children's homes were sometimes fifty or more miles away and the difficulties of regular visiting were very real. The same reasons for their being admitted to hospital in the first place often made it impossible for them to stay at home overnight.

I often thought that Dick, who spent Monday to Friday on Skylark and almost every weekend at home, got the best of both worlds. He had all the services of the hospital during the week – school, physiotherapy, dentistry – and all the love and comforts of home at the weekend. Dick was an only child of devoted parents whose comfortable home had been adapted to cope with a profoundly handicapped child. Dick was of very low-grade intelligence, with little sight, but he obviously 'knew' his parents, and would sometimes weep when they left him after bringing him back to the ward, or on the very occasional Friday when they were unable to pick him up.

Children who were visited once or twice a year did not seem to recognise their families, or to 'welcome' them, as did children like John, Hilda, Pamela and Lucy, who were visited more often. I very much admired the parents who ran the gamut of the ward to visit their child. Often they found it tremendously difficult to come and see *their* child, surrounded by so many other handicapped children. Sometimes, if they arrived unexpectedly, nurses would not be around to greet them, or to ask if they wanted to see their child in the visitors' sitting-room, the day-room or the classroom. I never found it easy to return to the ward after a two-week holiday. I would feel strangely embarrassed and reluctant to walk in. Little wonder that parents who did not come often found it a tremendously exacting experience. In a sense, the less often they came, the harder it was. Often I felt they needed help to know how to talk to their child, to make contact and to play with him.

Families usually visited at the weekends when school staff were not around. We met some parents at school open-days specially arranged for them, and I occasionally went in at the weekend to meet parents who had asked for this. When families visited during school time we had the opportunity to meet and talk and to offer different toys that we knew their child enjoyed playing with. In this way we got to know a few families very well. We were always encouraged by this friendship and the whole classroom enjoyed their visits as well as their own child.

CHRISTMAS ON THE WARD

During December the ward really came alive. It was a season when nursing staff could enjoy giving the children a good time. Immense trouble was taken to decorate the ward, to choose suitable presents for each child, and the climax came in a Christmas tea party to which all the families were invited. There was music, dancing, dressing up and a puppet show. Staff, parents and children had a magnificent tea together.

During this time staff morale rose, brightening the whole atmosphere of the ward for staff and children alike. My only reservation was about the tendency to overlook ways in which the children could be involved in the preparations. Here were opportunities for a child to hold one end of a paper

82

chain while the other was being fastened to the ceiling, to sit up close to the tree while it was being decorated, to sit on a nurse's lap while she wrapped presents. We gradually encouraged the nursing staff to help the children take their own cards from the envelopes, and to let them help, however slowly, unwrap their own parcels.

Nursing, school and physiotherapy staff worked together to get as many of the children as possible to the various pantomimes and Christmas parties that were organised elsewhere in the hospital, sometimes by groups of volunteers from local colleges. One year, some of us took six children to see a circus. The children enjoyed it tremendously, but the staff were distressed by the attitude of the parents of normal children who sat around us. Close proximity to a very handicapped child still makes many people fearful and anxious, as if being handicapped was in some strange way contagious. There were always exceptions to this, and on summer outings the understanding and kindness of some people, like shopkeepers, was touching and rewarding.

SUMMER OUTINGS

These were arranged for every ward in the hospital, four times during the summer months. Initially I felt it was an almost impossible undertaking to give each of thirty dependent people a good day on the same expedition. I pressed for smaller, more frequent, minibus expeditions with six to twelve children. But the hospital pattern was set on ward outings in a large, purpose-build coach, with a hoist for wheelchairs and built-in toilet facilities. We occasionally supplemented these all-day outings with shorter, smaller minibus trips, but the difficulties of finding enough staff and requisitioning the minibus made such trips rare.

On the positive side, there was a wonderful *esprit de corps* on the ward outings. Like Christmas, a ward outing, provided the staff with an opportunity to give the children pleasure, in ways they knew how to manage. Nursing staff

83

not on duty would volunteer to join in; school, physiotherapy, domestic staff and one or two volunteers would
swell the adult helpers until there was an almost one-to-one
relationship between adult and patient throughout the day.
Nearly everyone came in early so that we could leave at 10
a.m. and we were usually back about 7–8 p.m., exhausted
but happy.

The children loved the movement of the coach, and sitting
up high, many on an adult's lap, they looked out at the
traffic, the fields, the towns and villages we passed through.
The rhythm of the coach seemed to lessen, dramatically, the
incidence of epileptic fits during the day.

Where to go to was always a much discussed question. The
seaside was seventy miles away, and we never managed to
find a place that met all the needs of our particular group.
These needs included easy wheelchair and pushchair access
to a beach, clean sand with only a short distance to the sea,
nearby coach parking facilities with privacy for eating and
changing, and small shops and amusements for children who
did not particularly enjoy the beach or too much sun. We
took them to zoos, safari parks and aquadromes. The best
outing I went on was to a wooded, uncrowded children's play
park, which had a very large, shallow paddling pool. We
never managed to take them to a friendly farm or on a picnic
by a country stream, which I felt the children would have
enjoyed.

The children always seemed happy out of doors, provided
they were not too hot or too cold. Their individual responses
to the feel of natural growing things, to sights, sounds and
movement varied, but as a group their combined responses
to grass, leaves, flowers, moss, sand, rocks, stones, earth and
water in natural settings, to the sound of waves, wind in the
trees, birds singing, and to the warmth of the sun on their
bodies, was very evident. I would have liked 'outings' based
on two principles: a one-to-one relationship with an adult,
and a sustained effort to bring each child into touch with as
many natural sensations as possible.

84

In order to achieve a one-to-one relationship for even limited periods of time, it is necessary to recruit voluntary help. Efforts to do this, in recent years, have shown that it is possible and very fruitful to draw community help into hospitals, hostels and parent-based projects for handicapped children such as *Kith and kids*. There is fulfilment in this for both the helper and the helped.

The hospital had a full-time organiser of volunteers and a great number of people came to work voluntarily in the hospital. The majority were young people, recruited from youth groups, boys and girls doing community or social studies in their last year at comprehensive school, sixth-formers at grammar school and students from colleges. There were also some older people, from various walks of life, who had built up a relationship with a particular patient and came to help, consistently, once or twice a week for years. For staff this help and interest were invaluable. For a multiply handicapped person the arrival of a volunteer represented *at the least* another pair of hands and legs, someone who could take a wheelchair patient out for a walk, to a pantomime or on an outing. Often he was much more than that, taking time to establish a meaningful relationship with a child (see Geoffrey and Robert, page 26). The hospital, in fact, recruited a number of junior aids from the comprehensive school children who had first come to the hospital as volunteers. On the whole, we found that it was the mature student, or older person, who found it easier to make a relationship with the profoundly handicapped child.

TAKING CHILDREN HOME

Occasionally I took a child home for the day. When I did this I was acting not as a member of staff but as a volunteer. I learnt more about the children in a few hours at home than I

85

might in a year in the structured work setting. Looking after John at home for twelve hours gave me more insight into the nurses' work on Skylark Ward, and the burdens carried by parents of handicapped children, than anything else had done. It also taught me a lot about 'community' attitudes to profound handicap. In the same way as these children need 'an interpreter' in order to get through to the outside world, equally, people outside need 'an interpreter' to help them respond appropriately to the non-verbal person. When John or some other handicapped child came to the house, friends and neighbours loved to come in to talk and to play but they relied upon us, as a family, to give them a lead.

Before I started work in the hospital my husband and I and my three sons were all afraid of mental handicap, partly because we did not know how to act naturally with a mentally handicapped person. Over the years, my children gradually came into the hospital to work as volunteers, until it reached a point where they begged me to start bringing one or two children to our home. Once they understood how to relate to John and other children, it gave them real happiness to see them in our house.

As the result of a hospital 'One-to-One' day[1] an elderly couple who had looked after one of the most handicapped children on Skylark for the day, continued to come in twice a week to work with him and the other children in the classroom. Their dearest wish was to be able to take him to stay overnight in their home once they felt sufficiently confident that they could manage. When this happens, that couple will get as much out of the visit as the child.

It is no good writing white papers about 'community care' unless individual people, like that couple, actually want to befriend a particular mentally handicapped person, and do so.

FAMILIES WITH A HANDICAPPED CHILD LIVING AT HOME

It seems relevant to mention here the work that is being done in some places to identify, as soon as possible, the birth of handicapped children, and to bring help to their families as soon as possible. The whole emphasis, nowadays, is on early support for parents, early treatment and advice, and early physiotherapy and training.

A special clinic was held in our local district general hospital to which babies and young children could be referred by family doctors and the social services department. Here they were seen by a psychiatrist who was also a paediatrician, by a physiotherapist and other experts in child development. Early identification of handicap, or possible handicap was followed up with treatment. In addition, a workshop for parents of handicapped children was started, in order to work out detailed programmes of training which parents could follow at home, based on a similar course pioneered by the Hester Adrian Research Centre in Manchester.[2]

Parents in our area could also make use of an opportunity playgroup where handicapped and normal pre-school children played together, while support, advice and friendship could be offered to the mothers.[3] A toy library for handicapped children had been started in conjunction with the opportunity playgroup.[4] The people responsible for starting and running all these new services worked closely together to provide a service for families with a handicapped child at home.

Parents with a handicapped child often feel too overwhelmed to seek out the help they need. Where services are available it is essential that you, and I, as ordinary citizens, should pass on the good news whenever we come across parents who need support and special help.[5]

Chapter 9

VERY HANDICAPPED BABIES

After I had been on Skylark Ward a little while we took in a baby of eighteen months who had been perfectly normal until an attack of meningitis at a few months old. Her parents had a normal, highly intelligent, little boy of three. The baby, whom I will call Margaret, was constantly ill with respiratory infections, tremendously difficult to feed, and becoming increasingly contracted in all her limbs despite constant handling and physiotherapy. She occasionally seemed to rally slightly, and on two occasions as we nursed her, we thought we saw the flickering of a smile. For the rest of the time, unless she was asleep, she wailed piteously and seemed to be experiencing continuous pain and discomfort. She seemed to be destined for a life of unrelieved suffering. Time and again when she was really ill with a high temperature, the staff prayed inwardly that she and her family might be released from their agony. Again and again she lived for days at a time on massive dosages of drugs and nothing else.

Over the months she wasted down to a tiny, almost inert skeleton, her constant crying became thin and hoarse, her face was contracted with lines of pain even while she slept. Regularly, twice a week, the family came to see her and to sit round her cot – grandparents, parents and the little brother, Jonathan. During these visits Jonathan would come and play in the classroom and we used to plan his mornings so that children like John, Hilda, Pamela and Jane would, at least, provide him with an appreciative audience. Jonathan seemed to ignore their handicaps completely and played quite naturally amongst them. We used to have sand or water play,

88

painting, or tea parties in the wendy house. Jonathan's play and chatter delighted our Skylark children and we had happy mornings. But as the months lengthened into years, Jonathan became more and more strained and white, and one had the impression that in some extraordinary way this little child was 'carrying' his family's crisis. They never visited without him, and he never spent any time near Margaret's cot unless constrained to do so.

Finally, after two years with us, Margaret died. I shall never forget the peace on her face just after she died. We wept and we rejoiced. I never saw her family or Jonathan again. He was now five and had just started school which apparently he thoroughly enjoyed. I hoped fervently that he could leave the sadness of his early years behind him, but I wondered.

I was an observer, an outsider, in this story except that when she was well enough, Margaret came into the classroom to be nursed by us, and we saw quite a lot of her brother and her family. I was left with many questions unresolved.

On Skylark a number of people at the top of the hierarchy were committed to the work of keeping Margaret alive – the psychiatrist, the doctor, the charge nurse and the physio-therapist. The twenty-four hours a day work of washing, changing, feeding, nursing, caring for Margaret was mainly carried out by student nurses, untrained nursing auxiliaries and untrained junior aids. I often watched girls of seventeen spending an hour coaxing a little food or drink into Margaret. Margaret's life might have been termed 'unproductive' for her, but the loving response it evoked was very far from unproductive. Caring of this quality is one of the most 'productive' things in human living. Everyone on Skylark, including the cleaners and the school staff, were to some extent involved in Margaret's life, in the daily task of keeping her alive and as happy as they knew how. It was impossible to be part of that particular community and stand aside from the questions that her painful living presented hour by hour.

Since Margaret came and went, Skylark has received, for

varying periods of time, babies under two-years-old who are, and who will always be 'just alive'.

Anne's sudden death (see page 32) and the prolongation of Margaret's life, convinced me of the need for some kind of ward discussion group under the guidance of an experienced leader during which all members of the caring team could have an opportunity to voice the feelings, anxieties and questions, which they otherwise discussed, perhaps harmfully, among themselves.

The need for a legitimate, controlled and therapeutic outlet for staff anxiety and stress has been recognised in the hospital now by staff discussion groups and regular seminars on such questions as:

1 How far is it reasonable, and justifiable, to prolong with drugs the life of such a baby?
2 How far should the needs of the normal siblings be considered in this kind of situation?[1]
3 With whom should the responsibility for the cessation of drugs lie? Does our present society expect too much of a doctor in leaving the final decision to him?
4 Isn't it essential that all the members of a caring team, in this kind of situation, should have the support and outlet of guided, regular group discussion?[2]

WHO MAKES THE CHOICE?

It seems to me that our society has begun to explore two distinct, new areas about severely handicapped babies. The first is concerned with the increasing number of choices that are becoming available, about the 'committing to life' of profoundly handicapped people. The second is about the prolongation of life of such babies once they have been born.

In the first area, decisions about 'committing to life' of profoundly handicapped people is becoming less haphazard, less dependent on the personal decision of a midwife, and less controlled by the medical specialist who may have no further part to play in the life of the baby once it has been safely delivered.

For some handicaps, both physical and/or mental, genetic counselling is becoming available, in certain parts of some countries, for married couples who have been identified as likely to have, for instance, a child with cystic fibrosis, haemophilia or spina bifida. These couples on hearing the medical evidence of the likelihood of having a handicapped child, may decide to have no children, or no further children.

If a pregnancy has started, a mother who is likely to have a handicapped child can have tests, such as amniocentesis, which may confirm that the foetus she is carrying has some abnormality. Doctors can give the parents the medical evidence of handicap, or the likelihood of handicap, and the parents may decide to have the pregnancy terminated. It has to be remembered that the trauma of the effects of such parental decisions, made as a result of prenatal diagnosis, cannot be underestimated. The rate of progress in the field of prenatal diagnosis of some handicaps is phenomenally high. New and morally testing options increasingly and daily present themselves to prospective parents.

'The great victory of prenatal diagnosis is that it gives the option of preventing before birth the existence of certain wholly undesirable diseases. But it does more than that. It pushes the critical decisions which have to be made as a result of the newly available information out of the hands of doctors into the hands of patients, where they belong.'[3]

'The widespread application of science in our society has tended to centralise many important decisions into the hands of a few highly qualified people. Antenatal diagnosis is an outstanding counter-example to this principle. It allows ordinary people to take possibly the most important decision of all – namely, who should be allowed to be born. The consequences of antenatal diagnosis ... are profoundly democratic. The decisions that most of us will at least have to consider making, though, are not easy ones.'[4] There are many people with handicaps who lead happy useful lives. Not allowing them to be born would be our loss, and our collective democratic fault.

For a long time yet severely handicapped children will be born, and perfectly normal people will as a result of later accidents or infections be made profoundly handicapped, as was Margaret. This is the second area of choice about the prolongation of life of such people that we have to face. As the teacher on Skylark my role was clearly defined. I had charge of a group of children who had been committed to living, by a person or persons unknown, and it was my job, as part of a team, to help them with all available skills to achieve any potential they might have. But it would be dishonest to pretend that there were not very real differences between the lives that John, Hilda, Pamela and the other children already described might lead, and the future life that faced Margaret and her family.

Chapter 10

'HEARTBREAK WARD'?

One day I overheard two domestics discussing the ward, as they drank a cup of coffee in the canteen sitting-room.

'Where are you working now?'

'Skylark!'

'You know what they call Skylark? . . . heartbreak ward!'

'You never finish, do you? feed them . . . clean up the mess . . . and it's time to start getting the tea ready.'

'Heartbreak ward!' I sat there thinking. The two young women had expressed, exactly, the root of the frustration felt by most people who worked on that ward. Thirty totally dependent children and young adults, with very often only three or four nursing staff to cope with all their needs. A long day which started at 8 a.m. and went through to 9 p.m. with three half-hour breaks for meals. At the weekends, when there was no school or occupational therapy relief, it was thirteen hours of assembly line monotony, washing, feeding, changing, clearing up; washing, feeding, changing, clearing up. But this was not a factory assembly line where at the end of the day one had screwed a thousand bolts into a thousand pieces of a car – and perhaps earned good over-time money. We had been dealing with people, with human beings, whom *we* knew had to be treated differently from nuts and bolts, and yet *we* hadn't the time, or the skills, or the materials, to interact with them appropriately at a level that was humanising for them and *us*. The more understanding we had of these children's un-met needs, the greater the sense of personal inadequacy and frustration we felt, coupled, at the end of a long day, with total physical exhaustion.

One enterprising young student nurse weighed all the

patients and discovered that the gross amount was double that of all the totally dependent patients on the equivalent ward, Kestrel, and yet the staffing ratios were the same. Many of the people doing the lifting were young girls or older women.

Sometimes I went to Skylark on a Sunday morning to take John to the morning service in the hospital chapel. At 10 a.m. the children would all be in their wheelchairs waiting to be washed and changed – rocking, crying, eating their clothes, pulling at a next-door neighbour, dribbling, vomiting, protesting. Two weary girls would be gradually working through them, while the other two had gone for late breakfast. In the kitchen a domestic would be clearing up the remains of breakfast, and perhaps another would be cleaning the floor of the day-room where the children had just finished their meal. I would wash and change John into his best clothes and off we would go to chapel.

Out of doors it might be a beautiful March morning, with the sun shining on the lines of young green wheat, and the hedges just coming into bud. We would pause to listen to a blackbird pouring song from the top of a hospital lamp-post. In the hedge we would see an old bird's nest which I would pick out for John to hold. We would talk about the new nests soon to be made and the small blue eggs the hedge-sparrow would lay in them.

In the chapel there were some more able children from other wards, who had come under the care of a reliable adult patient. The young hospital chaplain, Hugh, would welcome us as we arrived: 'Hello John! good to see you . . . this is John, who's come up from Skylark!' John would beam his happiness, and kick his legs with joy. The wheezy organ sprang to life, and we would all sing, in our own ways, 'Onward Christian soldiers!' Patients who could not read would pass their hymn books to a member of staff, so that they could have the page opened at the right place. One schoolchild, who could read a little, would skip for joy, and point excitedly at an occasional word he recognised, like 'Why' and

94

'Where'. The prayers were simple and many could shout 'Amen'.

One morning, for the talk, Hugh told us a simple story about when he was a little boy of eighteen months, just able to toddle into the garden. After messing about with the rubbish heap and getting all covered in mud, he wanted to go back indoors and find his Mummy. But in the gateway sat a great black cat and he was afraid to go past. He cried. Suddenly his Daddy appeared and picked up the great black cat, and the little boy could go safely indoors. 'That is the way it is for us. Sometimes we are very frightened and worried about things, like that great black cat. Then God, our Father, comes and takes the frightening thing away, and we feel safe and happy again.' I glanced sideways at John who was laughing as the chaplain went on all-fours to imitate the big black cat. In the congregation there were many people suffering from mental illness. They had come from a nearby psychiatric hospital. Did the story help them, I wondered?

At the offertory, John put his coin into the bag, and grinned appreciatively, as the bored, tearful two-year-old son of the chaplain escaped from his mother and sat briefly on Hugh's surpliced lap.

At Communion, I would wheel John to the altar rail and with help he could consume a fragment of host and a sip of wine. His face was radiant. His hand would clasp mine as we sang the final hymn and began our slow walk back.

In the ward, the other children, all cleaned up, would be sitting in their wheelchairs in the day-room, waiting for dinner at noon. In the kitchen thirty plates were being loaded up with mince, chips and peas; thirty helpings of trifle were being doled out on to another trolley.

'Sit down a minute, Ann, have a glass of sherry, we've got half a bottle left over from Mrs J.'s Christmas present. I must have a fag before we start the dinners. I noticed it was a lovely day when I cycled home for my breakfast. . . . Have a biscuit . . . spoil yourself, it's Mother's Day after all.' Doris was short, stout, bespectacled, pink-cheeked, motherly with one professionally qualified daughter living away from home. She was divorced, lonely and always ready for a bit of fun. She smiled, offered me a tiny glass of sherry and a cigarette. 'Must get the weight off my feet for a few minutes. It's been all go since we started this morning. Had to bath Sam, clothes and all, he was filthy, it was everywhere, all over his face, in his hair . . . he stank' – and Sam could stink!

I remember Doris on the outing we had one summer, voluntarily looking after Tommy all day – the heaviest, most inert, unresponsive, adult patient on the ward. Tommy who never smiled, hideous, with a huge hydrocephalic head, dribbling all over you, clutching in a vice-like grip any part of a human being that comes within his reach. I have a snap of Doris, laughing, her hair ruffled, her spectacles askew, skirt pulled up high, holding Tommy, as they sit with their bare legs on the side of a paddling pool. She is splashing his legs with the water, encouraging him to enjoy the sun, the pool, the unaccustomed surroundings of a beautiful play park for children, ignoring the very obvious movement of normal families away from our end of the large pond. Probably she doesn't even notice them because she and Tommy and the rest of us are having such a good time. I also remember how, at the end of the day, when we had given the children a really good time and finally washed and tucked them all up in bed, a few of us went to the staff social centre for a glass of beer. Most of us had families and suppers to go home to, but Doris said 'No point my going home yet. . . . I'll stop and have another drink. . . . I'm on a long day again tomorrow.'

I came back to the present as Doris asked 'Did John enjoy the service, Ann? . . . made a lovely outing for him, anyway, on a day like this.' I told her how much he had enjoyed it, and rose to go. Time to get back to my own family. As I left I looked into the day-room to have a final word with John. All the children were grouped round, shrouded in sheets to keep their clothes clean – a few parents might visit in the afternoon. Doris and three others had started the long process of shovelling in the mince and trifle. John sat slumped in his chair, dejected – so different from the radiant child in the chapel. I felt I was running away. 'Bye Ann!' Doris waved, cheerfully, 'see you again soon'. How easy to give up three hours on a Sunday morning, but what difference had it made to John and to 'heartbreak ward' – a drop in the ocean of meaningless monotony?

But, did it have to be like this?

The answer, of course, is 'No!' But to change Skylark for the children and for the staff some radical thinking and action were needed.

Chapter 11

SKYLARK RENEWED

NURSE TRAINING

From my time on Skylark Ward, it was evident that many of the limitations in the children's way of life were recognised but were unalterable so long as the 'nurses' tried to just 'nurse'. In the same way, much of the staff dissatisfaction stemmed from their knowing that the children needed something quite different, most of the time, to 'nursing'.

'Each handicapped person needs stimulation, social training and education, purposeful occupation or employment, in order to develop to his maximum capacity, and to exercise all the skills he acquires, *however limited they may be*' (my italics), runs one of the guiding principles in the White Paper *Better services for the mentally handicapped*. Many of the nursing staff on Skylark realised, dimly or acutely according to their individual levels of thinking, that they needed to be moving away from a basically clinical nurse training to something much more like a special form of child caring with which they could meet the children's need for stimulation, social training and education, *throughout* the day and in every activity they undertook with and for the child.

It has to be recognised that people who are drawn to caring for the mentally handicapped are essentially different from those drawn to the ordinary nursing profession, in aims, ambitions and total outlook. Different skills are needed to care for the profoundly mentally handicapped, and different skills were being offered on Skylark but not finding an appropriate outlet.

Closely linked with the question of how to train people to look after profoundly handicapped children, was the lack of homeliness in the physical environment of Skylark Ward.

The first essential would seem to be an adaptation of the existing arrangement of the building. This would require imaginative thought, based on the real needs of patients and staff. In the present economic climate one would not recommend expensive rebuilding. Within two years of my leaving Skylark, the whole hospital was to be rearranged as a result of the opening of a new purpose-built school, situated within a few hundred yards of Skylark. This made it possible for any child of school age on Skylark to be wheeled into school, as had happened over the past few years for Kestrel children. When the new school opened, the classroom teaching on Skylark ended.

To make Skylark more homely the two vast day-rooms, and the four large dormitory areas would need to be subdivided into smaller units. With inexpensive partitioning and the use of varied floor covering, it should be possible to create an easily cleaned dining area, a sitting-room, a play area for messy activities like sand, water and paint, and a further play area with indoor hammocks, swings, simple indoor seesaws and possibly a small quiet room kept for music and individual play for children like John who would benefit from brief periods of one-to-one games and conversation.

Other subnormality hospitals have managed to upgrade their very old-fashioned dormitories and day-rooms. In a sense our hospital had a disadvantage in that it was only ten years old. Yet in many ways it was already out-of-date in the light of recent policy for severely handicapped people. Because the day-rooms and dormitories were spacious, sunny and nicely wallpapered, it seemed a less-important planning priority to break them down into smaller, more homely, areas, than if one were tackling some ghastly, Victorian 'Nightingale' ward or dormitory. But for the Skylark patients' well-being, some rethinking and rearrangement were urgent. In fact, in some ways, older buildings could be

99

made more homely when suitably up-graded. Someone in the hospital described a sitting-room she had seen in an up-graded old hospital where children were playing on a wall-to-wall carpet in front of a huge old-fashioned coal and log fire, surrounded by a completely safe fireguard, and said 'It all looked much cosier than the day-room on any of our wards.'

My heart bled every time I put John to bed after he had spent the day on an outing or in my own home. In the large, spotless dormitory with its gleaming modern tiled floor, there was nothing to mark out his bed, or his bed-space as his own. Beside his anonymous bed was a locker, marked with his name, issued under a regulation passed specifically as one of many recommendations to personalise the life of such people – but it was always empty. When John was in my ten-year-old son's bedroom he would look all round – at the posters on the wall, the goldfish, the canary in its cage, at the desk, the books, the half-made aeroplane models and at all the clobber that makes a person's room his own.

What a difference it would make to John's happiness, sense of belonging and feeling of personal identity, if he were to awake each morning surrounded by his own things – photographs of his parents, brother and sister, one of himself at the seaside, a mat on the floor by his bed, a small dressing table with a mirror before which he could sit to have his hair brushed and combed, a small wardrobe from which he could select the clothes he would like to wear that day and a drawer in which he could keep his letters from home, his postcards and his few favourite toys and personal possessions. John had a well-developed dress sense. I used to go shopping with him and he helped to choose some very attractive and suitable shirts and trousers for himself. In a more personal setting children like John would have renewed incentive to help dress and care for themselves. Staff looking after them would have the essential job satisfaction of fulfilling the children's obvious desires and preferences, instead of having to deny them or turn a blind eye to them, as they had to do several times each day in the current assembly-line method of washing, dressing and changing.

The arguments against the possibility of this kind of arrangement for severely handicapped people, on the grounds of staff shortage, are not convincing.

During the time I was on Skylark, one charge nurse had used his initiative to turn two little side-rooms into most attractive bed-sitting rooms for two of the ablest patients. But it was impossible for him to do this for more children without a restructuring of the main dormitories; there were simply no other small rooms available.

In the dormitories it should be possible to create some smaller units where children like John, who did not need minute-by-minute supervision from a nurse throughout the night, could share a bedroom with perhaps five other higher-grade friends.

Subnormality hospitals that have determined to break down the old institutional attitudes and methods of caring for patients in large groups, have had to make a start with perhaps one or two new 'family' units at a time.

At High Wood Hospital, Brentwood, I saw patients like the Skylark children, living in groups of twelve in what had been wartime nissen huts. Each hut had been divided into three main living areas, a dining-room next to the small kitchen, a living-room and a bedroom. There were movable screens dividing these areas, and each had a different floor covering. The bedroom had individual furniture and divan beds for the children and everywhere there was evidence of personal possessions. Here they had managed to recruit a number of part-time staff, who came in to work for a few hours at peak periods – such as getting up, going to bed and at meal times.

Once it has been decided, as a *matter of policy*, that the handicapped person can be allowed to act *at his own speed* with the minimum of adult intervention, the available staff can be fitted into that context. If a physical environment were created in which the handicapped person is motivated to do more for himself, the staff in attendance would find their work more meaningful and satisfying, they are more likely to come forward for employment, and more likely to remain once they are employed. On Skylark the nurse staffing ratio was too low for most of the time. The nurses' work was repetitive and meaningless and those who tried to use their initiative to do more for the children as individuals, were repeatedly defeated by the situation and they moved away to seek employment in more progressive units like the one at High Wood Hospital, Brentwood.

MEALS

Another way of tackling Skylark's problems might have been to reorganise certain wards in the hospital so that there was a more mixed ability range. By now, this may well have happened in that hospital. A grouping of patients in which some could do more for themselves, would have helped – particularly at meal times. Food, after all, can be a very real source of satisfaction. Attractively presented meals are the hub of happy family living. A few patients on Skylark could feed themselves and sit up at the table. Lunch would have been so different, I felt, if many more of the less able children had had their wheelchairs drawn up to attractively laid tables with a few staff members eating with them. In fact, a number of children who were always in wheelchairs for their meals were capable of sitting in ordinary chairs at low tables, even though their ability to feed themselves was very limited.

During my time on Skylark Ward, a short experiment took place in which two probationer clinical psychologists ran a three-month training programme for two children, who we felt might begin to learn to feed themselves. That experiment produced sufficient evidence on video-tape to suggest that given enough intensive training, more of the 'totally dependent' patients would, in time, learn to feed themselves.

Difficulties in achieving a self-feeding programme could have been reduced by:

1 Serving more food of a finger-feed variety – small sandwiches, small cakes, biscuits, fresh fruit, etc.

2 Careful grouping of patients round tables so that those who could do a little more for themselves could act as examples to those who were used to being totally dependent.

3 Less concern about the general mess such self-feeding would inevitably create; less emphasis on managing cutlery from the start; and less concern about the amount each child ate.

Each day there seemed to be a great waste of unappetising, mushy food. Often the children did not seem to be hungry because they were expected to eat three cooked main meals a day, with nothing like an ordinary nursery tea which they would have enjoyed and managed to eat with much less help. It seemed to me that the children would have derived more nourishment and enjoyment from various milk drinks, milk shakes, and bananas and ice cream (which they loved) than some of the unappetising mince with which they were so often faced.

These observations were reinforced by the behaviour of the children on ward outings, which I discussed in more detail earlier (see page 83). For these we took sandwiches and fruit, and we bought the children a variety of sweet biscuits, little chocolate swiss rolls, cup-cakes, ices, etc. It was amazing how much more they helped themselves than in the familiar ward setting; how quickly we could have a picnic compared to a ward meal; and most surprisingly of all, how very clean the incontinent children became for the day. There were, of course, some dirty nappies to change behind the coach, but many less than during a normal ward day. Because the surroundings were different, the children seemed, just for the day, to gain in morale and self-respect, and exhibit less of a need for dependence which the ward surrounding induced.

WARD PLAY PROVISION

Another aspect of Skylark living that needed fundamental rethinking was that of occupation for the children after school hours, during the three fortnightly school holidays in the year and at the weekends.

Structurally the provision of two or three smaller areas for play as indicated above would have helped. More essential, was the appointment of a play-leisure person, working all the day and evening hours when normal school staff and occupational therapists were not. Several hospitals have already made such appointments. Some very constructive efforts were being made in this direction when I left the hospital. They showed that it is not enough to provide good toys and play equipment, to set up hospital toy banks or libraries, or to recruit play volunteers, *unless* there is also a very active, imaginative person in charge of running and constantly revitalising the whole business.

At the end of school on Friday, Elizabeth and I had to pack away all the school toys and lock them in a cupboard. I hated doing this knowing that the children were going to face long hours of boredom until we were back on Monday morning. After I had been on Skylark a few weeks, a very enterprising nursing assistant, begged me, one Friday, to leave out some paints and brushes so that she could do painting with the children over the weekend.

'It's ghastly, Ann' she said, 'to be on a long day Saturday and Sunday, and have nothing to do with the kids.' I was delighted at her initiative and asked her to wash out the brushes and put them, with the paints, on top of the school cupboard when she had finished. I knew she was a responsible young married woman and would do as I asked. On the following Monday I saw several of the children's paintings pinned to the walls but no sign of the brushes or paints. The nurse had gone on a week's leave. After an intensive search throughout the ward I found the paint brushes, in various places, clogged with paint. I then realised I was lucky to find them at all. Half-an-hour's intensive washing got them clean, but the incident underlined for me the impossibility of expecting an overworked nurse to care for equipment in the way that I, as the person responsible for its continuing usefulness, would do, or as a specially employed weekend play leader would have done.

AN INTEGRATED SERVICE

Profoundly handicapped people need to live in a homely setting in order to be happy, and in order to develop whatever potential they may have. They need as much one-to-one attention with a caring adult as circumstances will allow. Once they have been trained to do a little more for themselves and are allowed to act at their own very slow pace, the one-to-one help can be slightly reduced and it can *supervise* rather than *act for* the handicapped person.

It seemed pointless to me to rush the children through the washing, dressing and changing process in order to be ready for school at 9 a.m., when, in school, one of the few things we could teach them was to be a little more independent. Stimulation, education and social training need to be given by *all* the staff, all the time. The old artificial division of functions between nurses, physiotherapists, teachers and other disciples seems meaningless when considering the needs of the profoundly handicapped. One can talk to a child while brushing his teeth and increase his awareness of himself more naturally in the bathroom than in the classroom. One can talk as naturally about colour as he eats a salad as by stacking coloured cubes in a playroom. It is more natural to encourage him to feel as he is tucked into cool sheets in bed, than by sitting him at a touch-board in the classroom.

The fun of involving these children in music and dancing, in laughter and playing, in watching birds feed and in lying on the grass should be shared by all the adults who look after them. As human beings whether we are the 'carers' or the 'cared-for' we all need a meaningful life. 'Our' needs and 'their' needs could be satisfied in an integrated service of loving care.

I have suggested in this chapter a few ways in which Skylark as a hospital ward might be made a better place to live in. I envisage it becoming much more like a hostel in which 'family living' in groups of not more than twelve handicapped people is introduced, with all the child-care staff acting *in loco parentis*, and, one hopes, with the child's own family visiting more often than at present.

Chapter 12

THE WAY AHEAD

In the last chapter I tried to suggest ways in which life could be made more satisfying and productive for the staff and children on one particular ward. As an extension of those suggestions I would like to indicate in this final chapter some of the projects which have been started in England, in recent years, which seem to merit serious consideration by anyone struggling with the problems of making a viable way of life for the severely handicapped and those involved in looking after them. Obviously it is going to take time, money and ingenuity before we can provide non-institutional care for all the severely handicapped people in our society. It remains as a goal to be worked towards.

Few would dispute that Auden's wish 'to be loved for oneself alone' is a common plea whether one is a handicapped person or just a person. Large institutions with a constantly changing flow of staff rule out the possibility of a one-to-one relationship between handicapped and normal people. Communities like L'Arche, the Camphill Village Settlements, the Rudolf Steiner schools and communities, where dedicated people live most of the time with their own families alongside handicapped people are unlikely to provide the final answer because of the insufficient numbers of ordinary people who can find such a way of life possible for them.

It seems to be a question of 'sharing the load' among the many normal people who can work wholeheartedly with the profoundly handicapped, provided they share this task with sufficient like-minded people and have enough time off in order to be able to return to their work refreshed by contact with life outside and with other interests. Very many parents would prefer not to hand their child over into total residential care provided they were given enough 'breaks' from the twenty-four-hour burden of looking after a very handicapped child or adult, and enough support and advice from other people with various skills in this field. The irrational guilt that many parents feel because they have borne a handicapped child is increased, not erased, when their family life breaks down under the burden they are carrying, and their child is admitted into permanent hospital care.

The Honeylands Family Support Unit in Exeter provides a network of help for families with a handicapped child to the extent that, since its inception ten years ago, very few children have had to be admitted to subnormality hospitals.[1]

Honeylands is an eighteenth-century mansion with spacious grounds in the centre of Exeter. Ten years ago it was decided to transform it into a family support and treatment unit for handicapped children. It is part of the pediatric department of the Royal Devon and Exeter Hospital and offers day and short-term residential care and treatment, and a twenty-four-hour-a-day telephone advisory service.

> It is open throughout the year. It is closely linked with the local educational, social, community and voluntary services as well as with the acute hospital service. The atmosphere is informal and no-one wears uniforms. Use of the day and short-term residential care and treatment service is both routine and flexible. Parents can establish a routine in which either or both of these services are used on a regular basis and they can also call upon them at any time for additional periods when they are needed, including crisis situations in their own families.
>
> This service is available for all children whose parents wish to use it, whether the child's handicap is predominantly intellectual retardation or physical disability. ... Optimal care and treatment of handicapped children requires special skills which have to be learnt and which call for considerable qualities of patience, endurance and tolerance. Often the acquisition of these skills has to be communicated to parents who are initially unprepared and ill-equipped to undertake such responsibility or for the adjustments that will need to be made to their daily lives.

108

Many professional disciplines are involved including medical, nursing, psychology, physiotherapy, speech therapy, occupational therapy, special education and sociology. The contributions of each of these disciplines to the treatment of an individual child have to be integrated into a practical daily routine.[2]

Anyone interested in the full implications of this project should read this article in full. Dr F. S. W. Brimblecombe, the consultant paediatrician in charge of the unit, has recently been given a grant by the National Fund for Crippling Diseases of £15,000, in order to evaluate the advantages of this family support unit. Further research is also going on at the Royal Devon and Exeter Hospital to evaluate the importance of following up babies admitted to the special-care baby unit of the hospital in order that any possibility of handicap should be immediately identified and treatment as well as family support brought in at the earliest possible moment.[3]

At Poole General Hospital, Dorset, Dr Ann Raikes, the developmental paediatrician, has worked to build a team approach to babies that have to be admitted to the special-care baby unit at Poole. 'The long term problems that may be encountered after such special treatments must not be forgotten and definite plans must be made for follow-up and support for such families after the discharge of the child. Difficulties in parental bonding, over-protectiveness, incorrect handling often follow prolonged separation and serious illness'[4] in the 'at risk' baby, who may, or may not, have been left with long-term handicaps.

At Loreto House, Bodmin, a home for twenty-four severely handicapped children was started in 1973 by the South-West Regional Hospital Board, where 'the children must remain the *raison d'être* for such a unit, not its justification'. Here, as at Honeylands, some cots and beds are retained for non-resident children on a programmed care basis.

One area in which valuable groundwork can be done is in the meticulous selection of staff. Everybody connected with the home must

109

understand, not only that a relaxed but therapeutic atmosphere is required, and what that atmosphere consists of. . . . Leadership is envisaged on a participatory democratic basis rather than an autocratic one. . . . Frustrations and problems receive a good airing and tensions which might otherwise reflect upon the children are given an opportunity to surface and be dispersed.

Most of the unit staff are nursing assistants, but their title is not seen to be important. The unit is staffed by people. The difference is subtle but crucial. These valuable members of the team are, initially, untrained, as emphasis is placed upon the selection of the right person, followed by relevant in-service training.

To minimize the possible adverse effect of multicare, the children are grouped so that each has a continuous, reliable and close relationship with a small number of nursing assistants, bearing in mind the necessity for 24-hour cover. . . . Catering assistants, ward orderly and portering staff are integral members of the family, spending a large part of their time with the children. Acknowledging this to be desirable has tapped an immense reservoir of compassion and patience, which has benefited the children enormously. Home is where everybody cares about you.[5]

What can be provided in Bodmin, Poole, Wessex (see page 38), Exeter, and other places mentioned in this book, in terms of really caring for profoundly handicapped people, must be possible in many more parts of this and other countries. What seems to be necessary is a person, or a team of people, with sufficient skill, vision and determination to find a good way of life for the profoundly handicapped and those who look after them. None of these pioneer projects have been provided initially by voluntary charitable organisations but are within the aegis of the National Health Service, drawing in many local sources of help and voluntary funds for extra volunteers and services.

POSTSCRIPT

When I left Skylark to take a class in the school building I wondered about John's relationship with his new teacher. I was very concerned that he might feel I had rejected him in favour of other children. I continued to go back to Skylark to take him to chapel, and I continued to take him home for the occasional day. Two very interesting things occurred after I left Skylark.

At the Christmas pantomine at the end of my first term away from Skylark, John sat in his wheelchair between his new teacher and myself. Although he was delighted to see me, it was to her that he looked for reassurance when the noise got very loud and he was a little frightened. It was clear to me that John had sized up the new situation and realised that his new teacher was his 'interpreter' to the outside world. I was one of his friends but she was his teacher.

At the next summer's One-to-One day (see page 86) someone took photographs of John and caught a picture of his face in complete repose. I had taken many photographs of him in my time but none of them had captured this expression of total serenity which I had seen on his face only in the chapel after he had received communion. It seemed to me that this confirmed what I had hoped for John more than anything else, that God through the sacraments had brought him a peace of soul that no human being could give him.

Nowadays when I take him to chapel and leave him back on the ward he looks peaceful, and not miserable because 'the outing' is over. And, yet, the following lines still haunt me.

'THE CAGED SKYLARK'

As a dare-gale skylark scanted in a dull cage
  Man's mounting spirit in his bone-house, mean house, dwells –
  That bird beyond the remembering his free fells;
This in drudgery, day-labouring-out life's age.

Though aloft on turf or perch or poor low stage,
  Both sing sometimes the sweetest, sweetest spells,
  Yet both droop deadly sometimes in their cells
Or wring their barriers in bursts of fear or rage.

Not that the sweet-fowl, song-fowl, needs no rest –
Why, hear him, hear him babble and drop down to his nest,
  But his own nest, wild nest, no prison.

Man's spirit will be flesh-bound when found at best,
But uncumbered: meadow-down is not distressed
  For a rainbow footing it nor he for his bones risen.

Gerard Manley Hopkins

Appendix 1

ASSESSMENT OF THE PROFOUNDLY HANDICAPPED CHILD

As indicated in chapters 4 and 6 of this book, the greatest difficulty facing anyone concerned with 'teaching' a profoundly handicapped child – and this person could be a parent, a nurse, a physiotherapist or a teacher – lies in establishing a base-line of this particular child's potential when the child is functioning at a level where formal testing procedures are impossible, or inapplicable.

Besides the need to establish a base-line, i.e. 'where do we begin?', there is also a need for something like the Gunzburg Primary Progress Assessment Chart, but adapted in ways which indicate the *very smallest* changes in the child's functioning.

Research at the Child Development Research Unit at Nottingham should be closely followed by anyone interested in this problem. Drs John and Elizabeth Newson and their research team have evolved new types of assessment linked with remediation based on play and the active involvement of the child's mother (see J. and E. Newson, Joan Head and Kay Mogford, *Toys and playthings in development and remediation*, Penguin – in press). I am greatly indebted to this team for their permission to quote one of their 'guideline' papers which they produce for the use of their own trainees.

SOME PRACTICAL GUIDELINES FOR THE TEACHING OF LANGUAGE TO NON-SPEAKING CHILDREN

This approach is grounded in a view of child development which tends to emphasise the importance of communication in the life of the ordinary normal human infant, particularly during the first year of life and certainly long before he produces his first understandable word. It is founded on the conviction that speech is symptomatic of pre-existing shared understandings between the infant and his regular human caretakers.

Kay Mogford has estimated that more than 85 % of the children referred to our Toy Library for Handicapped Children have speech and language problems. She has developed an interview schedule for

113

use with mothers, which enables a base-line to be established for communication skills in those cases where the child is functioning at a level below which formal testing procedures are possible (e.g. with the Reynell Test). The virtue of this instrument is that it relies on a mixture of different sorts of evidence including direct observation, maternal report and demonstrations of what the child does when interaction is attempted with the child.

In practice, then, we see a lot of children for whom it seems relatively pointless to ask 'How many words does he use?' or even 'How many words does he understand?' and we are thrown back on to asking 'How does he make his needs and wishes known?' and 'How do you persuade him to co-operate with you?' A large number of these children also have severe attention difficulties, so that the initial problem is to establish some kind of rapport with the child in order to ensure that at least he can share with another person common experiences, objects or points of reference. Whether one's aim is assessment or remediation (more often a progressive combination of the two), little can be accomplished until rapport can be achieved with the child. Our theoretical aim is, however, to unravel this mysterious process known as establishing rapport. In all social interaction, human beings emit signals to which other human beings are responsive. From the very beginning of life these include all kinds of gestures: gross bodily postural changes, hand and arm movements, changes in facial expression, head and eye pointings, vocal intonations, etc. It is the *temporal* patterning and interweaving of these actions in a reciprocally adjusted alternating sequence which underlies social rapport and leads to the creation of shared understandings. Even when spoken language is impossible, human beings are naturally well-equipped to enter into dialogues of reciprocally adjusted actions and hence to evolve shared codes of communication. And this is what every normal baby does with his mother during the first twelve months.

Precisely how language is learned in the ordinary course of normal child development is still a subject of fundamental theoretical controversy. The guidelines that follow are simply based upon an assumption that we should aim to reproduce, as nearly as possible, those optimal conditions and circumstances which seem so effectively to promote language development in the case of children without handicap. Obviously this is not a straightforward prescription because different forms of handicap will inevitably interfere in ways which can render the overall learning situation ineffective. Our efforts must therefore be directed towards compensation in the direction of normal communication, i.e. towards enabling the child to face the

114

task of learning to communicate in as near normal a manner as may be possible, bearing in mind the nature of his specific handicap.

The guidelines

1 To begin with we must expect that the communication codes which children evolve in interaction with other persons will be situation-specific and context-dependent. They will also tend to be heavily dependent upon the presence of one particular, familiar caretaker. The idiosyncratic codes which children tend to develop initially are nonetheless essential because they mediate genuine linguistic communication. In other words they provide a framework of shared understandings to which language can in time be attached. It follows that time taken in establishing non-verbal rapport with a child is never a waste of time.

2 In normal child development, language is first encountered as a kind of background music to familiar action sequences in which the child is caught up and fully involved as a participant. At this level words and phrases, like other intonational comments, are mainly important as 'markers' or as triggering and pacing signals accompanying a pre-established dialogue of actions. In practice, language as an intonational commentary will continue to have this function at the level of face-to-face interaction and its importance should not be underrated.

3 In the normal course of development, the understanding of language clearly precedes the active production of speech. This suggests the need for caution in the use of behaviour modification or other techniques to elicit active speech sounds from the child except in contexts where the utterance has reference which is self-explanatory to the child. In other words, eliciting techniques should not intrude to the extent that the child's utterances cease to fit into a natural two-way communication flow if this is at all possible. At the same time, there is room for intensive sessions designed to increase the volume and habit of utterance; backed by two-way interchange (or a simulation of it), these can act as interpreters to the child of the normal process.

4 Gestural and non-verbal cues in the dialogue of interaction probably need to be seen as supportive of the natural beginnings of communication at the verbal level. Here a distinction must be made between how we *test* for verbal understanding and how we devise an optimal *learning* strategy. When testing it is clearly necessary to exclude the possibility that the child is really responding to gestural and situational cues whereas in teaching they have an important facilitatory effect.

5 There is also a tendency when acting in the role of instructor to strip down the learning situation to its bare essentials on the grounds that this should make matters less confusing for the child. Yet in practice, children often seem to learn best in 'over-determined' situations where many different sorts of cues are available and there is an element of choice as to which cues the child will, in practice, utilise. Until we have more adequate theories about how human beings learn, the temptation to structure learning problems in terms of paradigms held by the instructor, but not the child, sometimes needs to be resisted: or rather, the instructor should be prepared to seize upon any paradigm which the child shows he can make use of, whether or not it is theoretically plausible.

6 If, as we believe, the evolution of shared understandings is essential to the later development of language proper, the implication is that it is inappropriate to view language acquisition as a process of transmitting 'knowledge' from an adult instructor to a child pupil. Shared understandings are a product of joint and reciprocal involvement between two persons. New understandings can only emerge on the basis of genuine reciprocity between two individuals, each of whom is allowed to take turns, i.e. to take the initiative in acting to sustain the dialogue. Neither partner is in complete control of the understandings which will emerge. It is also important that each participant quickly begins to share with his partner a whole history of successful past attempts to arrive at shared understandings; these may not be evident to the external observer whatever the sophistication of his observational recording equipment at a given point in time.

7 Communication between individuals is only sustained to the extent that it is intrinsically self-rewarding. Arriving at shared understandings is rewarding in and of itself, and the introduction of additional extrinsic rewards does not automatically result in an improvement in genuine two-way communication. Strategies based upon extrinsic rewards for specific acts of behaviour on the part of the child may actually eventually work against the evolution of those codes of communication which usefully lay the groundwork for spontaneous language development.

8 In the normal child, language evolves apparently effortlessly as a consequence of two-person involvement which is frequently game-like and humorous. Typically, well-worn interaction rituals develop which, once they are firmly entrenched, can become the focus for surprise or anticlimax should normal expectations be deliberately violated. At this stage, anticipation-teasing play can be initiated by either partner which introduces a lively and amusing

116

element into the dialogue and gives the child a vested interest in elaborating these two-person games so that they evolve and change before they have a chance to become predictable and boring. However, a minimum requirement for such productive learning-through-play is that the adult should put himself wholeheartedly at the disposal of the child, and probably a one-to-one relationship is important in the initial stages.

In 1958, John and Elizabeth Newson initiated their longitudinal study of child-rearing attitudes and practices in seven hundred Nottingham families. The study is unique in that it is following children from birth to twenty-one years – by which time many will have had their own children. Also it has been sustained throughout on the principle that if one wanted to know what people were thinking, feeling and doing, 'one might do worse than just ask them':

Newson, J. and E., *Infant care in an urban community*, Allen & Unwin, 1963
  Four years old in an urban community, Allen & Unwin, 1968
  Seven years old in the home environment, Allen & Unwin, 1976
  Perspectives on school at seven years old, Allen & Unwin, 1977

This research later extended to a special study of families with specific handicaps:

Hewett, S., Newson, J. and E., *The family and the handicapped child*, Allen & Unwin, 1970

The Child Development Research Unit is also undertaking the following research relating to handicap. Information and papers are available from University Park, Nottingham NG7 2RD.

SUPPORT FOR PARENTS

A major research interest in the Unit concerns remedial help for handicapped children, and strategies for helping parents to take their place as full members of the therapeutic team.

The Toy Library provides a service for the families of handicapped children by making assessments and offering advice on developmental problems. By lending carefully selected toys, and advising on ways in which they can be used, the potential of play as a medium for remediation is being realised, and parents are being involved in the remedial process. (Joan Head and Barbara Riddick)

117

Closely linked with the Toy Library project is a study of the ways in which the child's understanding and discovery of his world is influenced by the adult who participates in his play. What is learnt from the analysis of video-recordings of normal children is applied to understanding the effect that a handicap can have on his parent/child relationship, and will be used to suggest ways of improving counselling methods. (Kay Mogford)

Another study explores the use of behaviour modification techniques in the hands of parents of handicapped children, and the deliberate creation of a situation in which these parents are encouraged to make over behavioural strategies to suit the needs and circumstances of their own families and their own children. (Colin Pryor)

The parents of handicapped children frequently need support and guidance to help them to become a positive influence in their children's development. How can parents best be helped in the paediatric setting, and how can their continuing needs be fed back to doctors and social workers to ensure a flexible approach to the problem? This is a joint project with the Child Development Centre, Charing Cross Hospital, London. It will probably be extended into the 'family doctor' setting. (Rosemary Evans)

There is also a practical project concerning the language remediation of young mentally handicapped children in the classroom or at home. (Bill Gillham)

SPECIAL HANDICAPS

Specific handicaps pose their own problems. Previous work at Nottingham has been in cerebral palsy and visual handicap. Current projects are:

Deaf children

The parents of deaf children face difficulties in communicating with their children. How does this affect their handling of the child? How do they achieve their aims? (Susan Gregory)

A longitudinal study of deaf children and their communication patterns and strategies from the time of first referral onwards. (Kay Mogford and Susan Gregory)

A similar study of deaf children born to deaf parents. (Gill Hartley)

Down's syndrome (mongolism)

An analysis of interaction sequences between mothers and their mongol infants video-taped during play sessions at home is compared with

118

sequences between mothers and their normal babies. Differences in the development of mother–child communication in the two groups may point to the origins of some of the handicaps of mongol children and suggest possible remedial strategies. (Olwen Jones)

Early language development of mongols is compared with that of normal children, to throw light on the reasons for the slow growth of language in handicapped children. Ways of facilitating language in these children are also explored. (John Harris)

Autistic children

There is a single-case study of exceptionally sophisticated drawing competence in a young autistic child. (Lorna Selfe)

Another study concerns the social behaviour of autistic children in a school setting. (Derek Wilson)

Autistic children of normal intelligence are being studied in relation to their management and functioning in a social context. (Peggie Everard and Elizabeth Newson)

Appendix 2

SOURCES OF HELP

It is essential for parents of handicapped children, and professional workers in this field, to know what help is available. I strongly recommend the *Handbook for parents with a handicapped child* (1972), by Judith Stone and Felicity Taylor, Home and Schools Council, Case Publications, 17 Jacksons Lane, Billericay, Essex. Expanded version published 1977 by Arrow Books.

This book gives details of a very wide range of research centres, associations of professional workers and parent-founded self-help groups, and is divided into sections for easy reference. It is an invaluable, comprehensive guide to the many sources that are available in Britain. Without such a guide it is almost impossible to describe adequately the help available in terms of publications, services and groups. Mental handicap is a 'growth industry' in terms of campaigns, publications and parent groups for newly identified handicaps. After surveying the field one is left with the uneasy feeling that more co-ordination of effort and less overlapping of splendid goals, might lessen the gulf that still divides many unhappy, perplexed parents who, despite all the help that is obviously available, do not know where to seek it.

My selection of sources of help is an arbitrary one, related to the particular issues discussed in the book. Many of the centres and associations listed below have pamphlets written in terms which a layman can understand, and offer immediate practical guidance in both assessment and simple remedial programmes and activities for children who seem to be 'not quite right'.

L'Arche (homes and workshops for mentally handicapped adults), 21 Jubilee Place, London SW3 3TD.

British Society for Music Therapists, 48 Lanchester Road, London N6 (Tel. 01–883 1331). Free assessment sessions and will put parents into touch with music therapists. Publications on request.

Campaign for the Mentally Handicapped (CMH), 96 Portland Place, London WIN 4EX (Tel. 01–636 5020). An independent group started in 1971 as a pressure group and advisory centre for parent and local groups.

Apply with s.a.e. for details of local conferences, papers and 'Newsletter'.

Camphill Villages Association, 32 Heath Street, Stourbridge, Worcestershire DY8 1SB.

Child Development Research Unit, University Park, Nottingham NG7 2RD (Tel. 0602 56101). Currently producing research papers on many new ways to help children with varying handicaps (see Appendix 1 and Further Reading). Extensive reading lists are also available from their Toy Library.

Cottage and Rural Enterprises (CARE), Blackerton House, East Anstey, near Tiverton, Devon.

Handicapped Adventure Playground Association, 2 Paultons Street, London SW3 (Tel. 01–352 6890). Requests for latest information on plans for further playgrounds should be addressed to the secretary.

Hester Adrian Research Centre, The University, Manchester M13 9PL. Currently producing a series of books based on research with parents of handicapped children (see Souvenir Press publications listed in Further Reading). Cannot help with specific inquiries relating to individual problems.

Home Farm Trust, 57 Queen's Square, Bristol. Residential communities for handicapped school-leavers.

Institute for Research into Mental and Multiple Handicap, 16 Fitzroy Square, London WIP 5HQ. Initiates and co-ordinates research. Wide variety of publications, but cannot deal with parents' individual problems.

Invalid Children's Aid Association, 126 Buckingham Palace Road, London SW1 (Tel. 01–730 9891). Runs regular discussion groups for parents, with playroom for normal siblings. Publications and advice on request.

King's Fund Centre, 24 Nutford Place, London W1H 6AN (Tel. 01–262 2641). A forum for discussion of current problems. Conferences, projects, special 'pack' on mental handicap. Non-professionals welcomed to contribute to general discussions on mental handicap but not on personal, specific problems.

Music for Slow Learners Project (David Ward), Dartington College for Arts, Totnes, Devon (Tel. Totnes 2271 and 2527). Runs courses suitable for parents with minimum basic knowledge of music.

National Association for Mental Health (MIND), 22 Harley Street, London WIN 2ED.

National Association of Swimming Clubs for the Handicapped, 93 The Downs, Harlow, Essex (Tel. Harlow 25442). Register of swimming clubs for the handicapped.

National Association for the Welfare of Children in Hospital, Exton House, 7 Exton Street, London SEI 8VE (Tel. 01–261 1738). Information and advice to parents on 'long-stay' hospitals.

National Children's Bureau, 8 Wakley Street, Islington, London ECIV 7Q. Several books and pamphlets on many aspects of mental handicap are available on application. Requests for advice should be addressed to the information officer.

National Development Group for the Mentally Handicapped, Room C412, Alexander Fleming House, Elephant and Castle, London SEI 6BY. Set up in February 1975 to advise the government on mental handicap and on its implications. 'Although the Group works very closely with the Department of Health and Social Security, it is a body which has a considerable measure of independence.' The group is issuing a series of pamphlets, obtainable on application, on services for mentally handicapped people and their families. Thoroughly recommended: *Mentally handicapped children: a plan for action*, Pamphlet no. 2, March, 1977. Available from the secretary.

The Development Team for the Mentally Handicapped at the same address is complementary to the Group. Provides advice to field authorities about the planning and operation of services. Requests for advice should be addressed to the secretary.

National Society for Mentally Handicapped Children (NSMHC), Pembridge Hall, 17 Pembury Square, London W2 4EP (Tel. 01–229 8941). Has over four hundred affiliated local societies and twelve regional offices. Wide range of services and residential homes for mentally handicapped and multiply disabled people. Very wide range of publications, including a new booklist on 'Stimulation through play in early childhood'. Mailing list subscription: 50p p.a. Quarterly publication: *Parents Voice*, £1.50 p.a. Runs 'Gateway Clubs' for young adults throughout Britain.

National Fund for Research into Crippling Diseases, Vincent House, Springfield Road, Horsham, West Sussex, RH12 2PN (Tel. 0403 64101). Promotes research in hospitals throughout the country into causes, prevention, cure and treatment of crippling diseases. Excellent list of publications and quarterly journal *Action*.

Remedial Drama Centre, 602A Holloway Road, London N19 (Tel. 01–272 3137). Works in schools with ESN and maladjusted children. Runs training courses.

Riding for the Disabled Association, National Equestrian Centre, Kenilworth, Warwickshire (Tel. Coventry 27192). List available of organisations throughout the country.

Rudolf Steiner Schools, Rudolf Steiner House, 35 Park Road, London NW1. Guide to their schools throughout Britain.

Spastics Society, 12 Park Crescent, London WIN 4EQ, administrative headquarters; also 16 Fitzroy Square, London WIP 5HQ (Tel. 01–387 9571). Family Services and Assessment Centre. Runs an assessment service for parents of a handicapped child, and an information service on publications and equipment for the handicapped.

Thomas Coram Research Unit, Institute of Education, London University. Research based on the Thomas Coram Children's Centre and Hornsey Centre for severely handicapped children and adults (see Souvenir Press publications listed in Further Reading).

Toy Libraries Association, Sunley House, 10 Gunthorpe Street, London E1 7RW. Non-commercial centres for lending the best – and some specially designed – toys to handicapped children. Counselling service for parents on child's developmental needs in play and toys. Recent rapid expansion indicates its practical value to parents. Pamphlets available.

NOTES TO THE TEXT

CHAPTER 2: THE CHILDREN (pages 6–8)

[1] The children were assessed in comparison with normal children, and as a rough guide their functional age ranged from one month to two years eight months (see John, page 9), with the majority around the one year level.

CHAPTER 3: PROFILES (pages 9–33)

[1] J. J. Deacon, *Tongue-tied*, no. 8 in the series *Subnormality in the seventies* (NSMHC). £1.
[2] Five Shell Nature Records, 7 inch, 33⅓ r.p.m. including 'Fields and open countryside', 'Marsh and riverside', 'Estuary' and 'Moor and heath birds', by Shell Mex & BP Ltd, Discourses Ltd, 21 Manchester Square, London WI; 'Sounds of the countryside', narrated by Johnny Morris, mono, 45 r.p.m., and 'Bird sounds in close-up' by Victor C. Lewis, LP, Pye Records (Sales) Ltd, ATV House, Great Cumberland Place, London WI.
[3] Educational Supplies Association, Harlow, Essex.
[4] Play Pax, designed by Patrick Rylands, RCA, from Trendon Ltd, Malton, Yorkshire.
[5] Riding for the Disabled Association, National Equestrian Centre, Kenilworth, Warwickshire.
[6] The L'Arche organisation (see page 120).
[7] Mary Green, *Elizabeth* (Hodder & Stoughton, 1966); Hannah Mussett, *The untrodden ways* (Gollancz, 1975).
[8] Clare Claiborne Park, *The siege* (Pelican, 1967); Elizabeth Browning, *I can't see what you're saying* (Elek, 1972); Robin White, *Be not afraid* (Bodley Head, 1972).

CHAPTER 4: CHILD-BASED PROGRAMMES (pages 34–42)

[1] Mary D. Sheridan, Children's Developmental Progress, NFER Publishing Co, 1975.
[2] 'Evidence to the Committee of Inquiry into Mental Handicap Nursing and Care,' *Research report* from the Health Care Evaluation Research

Team (July 1976), Dawn House, Sleepers Hill, Winchester, Hampshire.
3 David J. Eden, *Mental handicap: an introduction* (Allen & Unwin, 1976).
4 J. Newson, *et al.*, 'Towards a theory of infant understanding', *Bulletin of the British Psychological Society*, 27 (1974) 251–7; J. Newson and John Shotter, 'How babies communicate', *New Society*, 8 August 1974.
5 Penelope Leach, *Babyhood* (Pelican, 1975), page 88.
6 B. Clarke, *Enough room for joy* (Darton, Longman & Todd, 1974) – an account of the L'Arche organisation, started ten years ago, which now has houses in France, Canada, Denmark, Scotland, Belgium, Bangalore, Calcutta and Bouake in the Ivory Coast. The English address is The Old Rectory, Little Ewell, Barfestone, Kent (Tel. 304 830 930); A. Shearer, 'An ark for survival', *New Society*, 13 March 1975.

CHAPTER 5: HOW THE TEAM WORKED (pages 43–53)

1 Nancy R. Finnie, *Handling the young cerebral palsied child at home* (Heinemann, 1974).
2 Copies can be purchased from the National Children's Home, 85 Highbury Park, London N5 (Tel. 01–226 2033).
3 Susan Thompson, 'Bridging the cultural gap', *New Psychiatry*, 17 October 1974.

CHAPTER 6: THE CHILD'S AWARENESS OF 'SELF' (pages 54–67)

1 Finnie, *Cerebral palsied child at home*, page 201.
2 Reproduced in *Aids for the handicapped* (Spastics Society, 1973). See also M. Ryan, *Feeding can be fun: advice on feeding handicapped babies and children* (Spastics Society, 1977).

CHAPTER 7: GROUP ACTIVITIES (pages 68–78)

1 The Nordoff–Robbins Music Therapy Council, c/o the Goldie Leigh Hospital, Lodge Hill, Abbey Wood, London SE2 0AY.
2 'Captain Noah and his floating zoo' (Michael Flanders and Joseph Horovitz), Argo record, ZDA 149.

CHAPTER 8: THE WIDER WORLD (pages 79–87)

1 A hospital carnival day, promoted to introduce people as volunteers to subnormality hospitals, One-to-one, c/o The Spastics Society, 76 Cambridge Road, Kingston-upon-Thames, Surrey KT1 3LB (Tel. 01–549 5988).
2 C. C. Cunningham and D. M. Jeffree, *Working with parents*, NSMHC, 1 Brazenose Street, Manchester M2 5FJ, £1.

³ For a list of Opportunity Playgroups write to the Pre-School Playgroups Association, Alford House, Aveline Street, London SE11 5DH.

⁴ For a list of local libraries and publications, write to the Toy Libraries Association, Sunley House, 10 Gunthorpe Street, London E1 7RW.

⁵ Liz Cooper and Roberta Henderson, eds. *Something wrong?* By parents of mentally handicapped children (Arrow Books, 1973); Charles Hannam, *Parents and mentally handicapped children* (Pelican, 1975).

CHAPTER 9: VERY HANDICAPPED BABIES (pages 88–92)

¹ Stephen Kew, *Handicap and family crisis* (a study of the siblings of handicapped children) (Pitman, 1976); Lindy Burton, *The family life of sick children* (a study of families coping with cystic fibrosis) (Routledge & Kegan Paul, 1975).

² Sula Wolff, *Children under stress* (Allen Lane, Penguin Press, 1969), particularly the chapters on illness and going to hospital, and on bereavement.

³ Robert Reid, 'The genetic chance', *The Listener*, 9 December 1976.

⁴ Fisher Dilke, 'A small imperfection', *The Listener*, 23/30 December 1976.

CHAPTER 12: THE WAY AHEAD (pages 107–10)

¹ See *British Medical Journal*, 4 (1974) 706, for a technical exposition of its work.

² F. S. W. Brimblecombe, 'Honeylands; a project for handicapped children', *Action Magazine*, September 1976. Obtainable from the National Fund for Crippling Diseases, Vincent House, 1 Springfield Road, Horsham, Surrey RH12 2PW, 25p; 'Before the bough breaks', a film about Honeylands by Glaxo–Farley Foods Ltd, for hire for £5 from The Film Services Library, Glaxo–Farley Foods Ltd, Torr Lane, Plymouth, Devon PL3 5GA.

³ F. S. W. Brimblecombe and M. P. M. Richards, eds., *Early separation and special care nurseries* (Heinemann – in press).

⁴ Paper by Dr A. Raikes at the conference on 'Parents, children and special care', National Association for the Welfare of Children in Hospital (London, November 1976).

⁵ P. Charlton, R. Fell and A. Henshall, 'Loreto House; a pattern of care', *Child care, Health and Development*, 1.3 (1975) 191–6.

FURTHER READING

EDUCATION

Since a baby, whether normal or handicapped, can start to learn from his earliest moments of life, the books recommended in this section refer to 'education' in the narrower sense of the term. They deal with the handicapped child of school-age. Several books in the section on 'Handicap and home life' are about teaching skills that will go on being taught by the special school.

Berry, P., ed., *Language and communication in the mentally handicapped*, Arnold, 1976

Carr, J., *He'll learn if we teach him* (in press)

Deich, R. F. and Hodges, P. M., *Language without speech*, Souvenir Press, 1977

Dixon, J., *Cued speech* (for severely deaf children), Souvenir Press, 1977

Education & Science, Dept. of, *Educating mentally handicapped children*, Education pamphlet no. 60, Her Majesty's Stationery Office

Fenn, G., *The development of syntax in a group of severely subnormal children* (in press)

Gunzburg, H. C., *Rehabilitation of the mentally subnormal*, Baillière, Tindall & Cox, 1960

Hannam, C., *Young teachers and reluctant learners*, Penguin, 1971

Kephart, N. C., *The slow learner in the classroom*, C. E. Merrill, 1971

McDowall, E. B., *Teaching the severely subnormal*, Arnold, 1964

McMaster, J. McG., *Towards an educational theory for the mentally handicapped*, Arnold, 1973

Marais, E. and M., *Lives worth living*, Souvenir Press, 1976

Peel, E. A., *The psychological basis of education*, Oliver & Boyd, 1956

Perry, N., *Teaching the mentally retarded child*, Columbia University Press, 1960

Segal, S. S., *No child is ineducable*, Pergamon, 1967

Standing, E. M., *Maria Montessori; her life and work*, Mentor-Omega, 1962

Stevens, M., *Observing children who are severely subnormal*, Arnold, 1968
    The educational needs of severely subnormal children, Arnold, 1971

Art

Tilley, P., *Art in the education of subnormal children*, Pitman, 1975

Music

Alvin, J., *Music for the handicapped child*, OUP, 1965
Dickinson, P. J., *Music with ESN children*, NFER Publishing Co., 1976
Hunt, A., *Listen – let's make music*, Bedford Square Press, 1976
Ward, D., *Hearts and hands and voices*, OUP, 1976

COMMUNITY CARE

Baranyay, E. P., *The mentally handicapped adolescent*, Pergamon, 1971
Bone, M., Spain, B. and Martin, F. M., *Plans and provision for the mentally handicapped*, Allen & Unwin, 1972
Brimblecombe, F. S. W., 'Honeylands; a project for handicapped children', *Action Magazine*, September, 1976
Clarke, B., *Enough room for joy* (an account of the L'Arche organisation), Darton, Longman & Todd, 1974
Charlton, P., Fell, R. and Henshall, A., 'Loreto House; a pattern of care', *Child care, Health and Development*, 1.3 (1975) 191–6
Forrest, A., Ritson, B. and Zealley, A., eds., *New perspectives in mental handicap*, Churchill Livingstone, 1973
Gunzburg, H. C., *Social competence and mental handicap*, Baillière, Tindall & Cox, 1973
Health Care Evaluation Research Team, Wessex Regional Health Authority, *An analysis of objectives in caring for the mentally handicapped*, July 1976
O'Connor, N. and Tizard, J., *The social problem of mental deficiency*, Pergamon, 1965
O'Gorman, G., *Modern trends in mental health and subnormality*, Butterworth, 1968
Shearer, A., *No place like home*, CMH Discussion Paper no. 5, 1975
Shennan, V., *The road to community care*, NSMHC, 1974
Stephen, E., ed., *Residential care for the mentally retarded*, Pergamon, 1970
Tizard, J., *Community services for the mentally handicapped* (an account of the Brooklands experiment), OUP, 1964

REARING A HANDICAPPED CHILD

Browning, E., *I can't see what you're saying* (the life of a boy with acute aphasic problems), Elek, 1972

Cooper, E. and Henderson, R. eds., *Something wrong?* By parents of mentally handicapped children, Arrow Books, 1973

Copeland, J. and Hodges, J., *For the love of Ann;* the true story of an autistic child, Arrow Books, 1973

De Vries-Kruya, T., *Small ship, great sea* (the life of a child with Down's syndrome), Collins, 1971

Deacon, J. J., *Tongue-tied; fifty years of friendship in a subnormality hospital* (the autobiography of a spastic man), no. 8 in the series *Subnormality in the seventies*, NSMHC, 1974

Green, M., *Elizabeth*, Hodder & Stoughton, 1966

Hannam, C., *Parents and mentally handicapped children* (the accounts of seven families), Pelican, 1975

Hunt, N., *The world of Nigel Hunt: the diary of a mongoloid youth*, Darwen Finlayson, 1967

Kaufman, B. N., *To love is to be happy with – the miracle of one autistic child*, Souvenir Press, 1976

Mussett, H., *The untrodden ways*, Gollancz, 1975

Park, C. C., *The siege* – (the battle for communication with an autistic child), Pelican, 1967

Roberts, N. and B., *David*, John Knox Press, 1968

Van der Hoeven, J., *Slant eyed angel*, Colin Smythe, Gerrards Cross, 1968

Van Houten, N., *Bartje, my son*, Hodder & Stoughton, 1960

West, P., *Words for a deaf daughter*, Gollancz, 1969

White, R., *Be not afraid* (the story of a boy who became brain-damaged), Bodley Head, 1972

Wilks, J. and E., *Bernard – bringing up our mongol son*, Routledge & Kegan Paul, 1974

HANDICAP AND HOME LIFE

Brutten, M. and Richardson, S., *Something's wrong with my child*, Macdonald, 1975

Burton, L., *Vulnerable children*, Routledge & Kegan Paul, 1968

Burton, L., ed., *Care of the child facing death*, Routledge & Kegan Paul, 1974

Burton, L., *The family life of sick children*, Routledge & Kegan Paul, 1975

Carlson, B. W. and Ginglend, D. R., *Play activities for the retarded child*, Baillière, Tindall & Cox, 1962

Collins, M. and D., *Kith and kids* (self-help for families of the handicapped), Souvenir Press, 1976

Cunningham, C. C., *Handling your handicapped baby*, Souvenir Press, 1977

Egg, M., *When a child is different*, Allen & Unwin, 1967

Field, A., *The challenge of spina bifida*, Heinemann, 1970

Finnie, N. R., *Handling the young cerebral palsied child at home*, Heinemann, 1974

Fox, A. M., *They get this training but they don't really know how you feel* (a 'consumer' study by families with handicapped children), Action Research for the Crippled Child, 1976

Freeman, P., *Understanding the deaf/blind child*, Heinemann, 1975

Gregory, S., *The deaf child and his family*, Allen & Unwin, 1976

Let me play, Souvenir Press, 1977

Teaching the handicapped child, Souvenir Press, 1977

Hewett, S., Newson, J. and E., *The family & the handicapped child* (a study of cerebral palsied children in their homes), Allen & Unwin, 1970

Jeffree D. M. and McConkey, R., *Let me speak* (a teaching programme for parents to help develop language skills), Souvenir Press, 1976

Kew, S., *Handicap and family crisis*, Pitman, 1976

King's Fund Centre, *Services for mentally handicapped children*, Paper 10, King's Fund, 1976

Kiernan, C., Saunders, C. and Jordan, R., *Teaching the first steps in development*, Souvenir Press, 1977

Newson, J. and E., Head, J. and Mogford, K., *Toys and playthings in development and remediation*, Penguin (in press)

Oswin, M., *Behaviour problems amongst children with cerebral palsy*, Wright, 1967

Russell, P., *The wheelchair child*, Souvenir Press, 1977

Ryan, M., *Feeding can be fun: advice on feeding handicapped babies and children*, Spastics Society, 1977

Sheridan, M. D., *The handicapped child and his home*, National Children's Home, 1973

Spain, B. and Wigley, G., eds., *Right from the start; a service for families with a young handicapped child*, NSMHC, 1975

Spastics Society, *Aids for the handicapped*, 1973

Stone, J. and Church, J., *Childhood and adolescence*, Random House, 1968

Stone, J. and Taylor, F., *A handbook for parents with a handicapped child*, expanded edition, Arrow Books, 1977

Tizard, J., *The mentally handicapped and their families*, OUP, 1961

Voysey, M., *A constant burden – the reconstitution of family life*, Routledge & Kegan Paul, 1975

SEXUAL AND SOCIAL NEEDS

Greengross, W., *Entitled to love*, Malaby Press, 1976

Mattinson, J., *Marriage and mental handicap*, Duckworth, 1970

Shearer, A., *A right to love?* (a report on public and professional attitudes towards the sexual and emotional needs of handicapped people), Spastics Society, 1972

Tudor-Davies, E. R., ed., *New prospects for retarded citizens*, NSMHC, 1975

The NSMHC (address on page 122) have issued a number of pamphlets in the last two years on this subject.

GENERAL

Carter, C. O., *Human heredity*, Penguin, 1970

Clarke, A. and A. D. B., eds., *Mental deficiency; the changing outlook*, Methuen, 1975

Clarke, A. D. B., *Recent advances in the study of subnormality*, MIND, 1975

Cowie, V. A., *A study of the early development of mongols*, Pergamon, 1970

Eden, D. J., *Mental handicap – an introduction*, Allen & Unwin, 1976

Furneaux, B., *The special child*, Penguin, 1973

Gardner, W. I., *Behaviour modification in mental retardation*, London University Press, 1971

Gingras, G., *Fighting for survival*, Souvenir Press, 1977

Heaton-Ward, W. A., *Mental subnormality* (the standard students' and nurses' handbook), Wright, 1967

Her Majesty's Stationery Office, The Education (Handicapped Children) Act 1970

Help for handicapped people, Leaflet HB1, Dept. of Health & Social Security and Welsh Office

Better services for the mentally handicapped, Cmnd. 4683, 1971

Human genetics (a list of every genetic advice centre in Britain), 1972

Hermelin, B. F. and O'Connor, N., *Speech and thought in severe subnormality*, Pergamon, 1963

Psychological experiments with autistic children, Pergamon, 1970

Kershaw, J. D., *Handicapped children*, Heinemann, 1966

Kirman, B., *The mentally handicapped child*, Nelson, 1972

Mental handicap: a brief guide, Crosby Lockwood Staples, 1975

Lagos, J. C., *Help for the epileptic child*, Macdonald, 1975

Lane, H., *The wild boy of Aveyron*, Allen & Unwin, 1977

Mittler, P., ed., *Assessment for learning in the mentally handicapped*, Churchill Livingstone, 1973

National Development Group, *Mental handicap; planning together*, Pamphlet no. 1

O'Gorman, G., *The nature of childhood autism*, Butterworth, 1970

Oswin, M., *The empty hours – the weekend life of handicapped children in institutions*, Penguin, 1973

Pilling, D., *The handicapped child; research review*, vol. 3, Longman in association with the National Children's Bureau, 1973. Out of print but available from the Bureau (address on page 122)

Rimland, B., *Infantile autism*, Methuen, 1965

Rutter, M., ed., *Infantile autism; concepts, characteristics, treatment*, Churchill Livingstone, 1971

Weston, P. T. B., ed., *Some approaches to teaching autistic children*, Pergamon, 1965

Wing, J. K., ed., *Early childhood autism*, Pergamon, 1966

BOOKS FOR CHILDREN

Jessel, C., *Mark's wheelchair adventures*, Methuen, 1975, suitable for ten-year-olds and upwards

Larsen, H., *Don't forget Tom* (a mentally handicapped child), A. & C. Black, 1974 and John Day

Peter, D., *Claire and Emma* (two deaf children), A. & C. Black, 1977 and John Day

Petersen, P., *Sally can't see*, A. & C. Black, 1977 and John Day

White, P., *Janet at school* (a child with spina bifida, in a wheelchair much of the time), A. & C. Black, 1977 and John Day

INDEX